THE HIDDEN SHAME OF THE CHURCH

Sexual Abuse
of Children
and the Church

Ron O'Grady

Risk
BOOK SERIES

WCC Publications, Geneva

Other books by the same author:

In the Risk Book Series

1979 – **Bread and Freedom,** on human rights
1981 – **Third World Stopover,** on tourism

On child sex abuse

1992 – **The Child and the Tourist**
(also in German, Japanese, Swedish, Vietnamese and Italian)
1994 – **The Rape of the Innocent**
(also in Singhala, French, Dutch, German, Japanese and Vietnamese)
1996 – **The ECPAT Story**
(also in Spanish)

Biblical quotes taken from the New Revised Standard Version of
the Bible © NCCC/USA
Cover design: Rob Lucas
Cover photo: WCC/Peter Williams

ISBN 2-8254-1349-6

© 2001, WCC Publications, the publishing division of the
World Council of Churches
150 route de Ferney, P.O. Box 2100
1211 Geneva 2, Switzerland
Website: http://www.wcc-coe.org

No. 94 in the Risk Book Series

Printed in Switzerland

Contents

Introduction

This book is written with a curious mixture of anger and sadness.

For the past eleven years my life has been focused on an organization dedicated to ending child prostitution, child pornography and child trafficking. The organization is an international coalition called ECPAT, now operating in more than fifty countries. In order to be effective it is strictly non-partisan in religion and politics. Consequently, my Christian beliefs have often been submerged behind a broader humanitarianism which motivates people of all creeds and races to protect children from those who would abuse them.

In the course of these eleven years I have encountered directly or indirectly a considerable number of men who have been child sex abusers. Included in this number have been several church leaders; at least three of them had been personal friends and colleagues in the ministry. The shock at discovering their secret life was compounded by the cynical way they have used the church to carry out their abuse and their subsequent attempt to justify their crimes.

Throughout my years with ECPAT I put clippings and notes related to clergy abuse in a special file, which began to bulge at the seams. The request from the World Council of Churches to write this book made me return to the file and re-read these stories of this last decade.

There was anger as I recalled the duplicity of some of these offenders and the suffering they had caused through their premeditated criminal actions. And there was sadness that an institution which promised so much in the way of spirituality and hope had become for many young people a place of despair and the destruction of their dreams.

I found it necessary to remind myself that while there are many shocking stories of clergy who have sexually abused children, these men are not typical of clergy in general. Those who lead the church are, for the most part, kindly and benevolent people who genuinely try to make the world a better place by being helpful to others.

However, ordination does not make clergy immune from human sin and those who become priests and pastors experience the same sexual drives as other people. With a few of them, the strength of their internal sexual urge has over-ridden their Christian values and led them to commit crimes against children which they have then tried to keep hidden from the church and the community.

How then can we discuss such stories in a rational and helpful manner?

This is the fourth book I have written on child sex abuse. In the first, *The Child and the Tourist*, written ten years ago, many of us had just come to understand the fearful dimensions of child sex abuse and we were deeply distressed. Especially shocking at that time was the brutal death of a young street girl, Rosario Baluyot, who was sexually abused and brutally killed by an Austrian medical doctor, a regular paedophile tourist to the Philippines.

Hearing about the incident affected me so much that I researched the story thoroughly and gave a full and graphic account of the abuse in the book, in the belief that it would shock others as well. There were many differing reactions. Some were stunned by the account and immediately moved to take action to end child abuse. Naturally, that was the result I had expected and wanted. But at least three people told me they had got part way through the story and had been so overcome that they couldn't read any more and closed the book. One of these three readers was a university professor.

But the most unexpected and shocking of all the reactions was the report of a sympathetic police officer, who said he discovered that the story of Rosario had been photocopied and circulated among some child sex offenders in prison. Far from being shocked by the account, the abusers found it exciting, stimulating and erotic.

Anyone working in the area of child sex abuse and want-ing to convince people of its serious nature knows this con-tinuing dilemma. How can we communicate the terrible facts of abuse in a manner which will neither paralyze some peo-ple and make them incapable of action, nor be used by others as a form of perverted pornography?

Learning from these experiences, I have since tried to take a middle way and provide information that will be shocking enough to move the reader to take some positive action but not so shocking that they will be paralyzed. This is another way of saying that anything you read in this book will be mild compared with some of the stories which could be told.

Many people in the church will not want to hear even these stories. Their perception of church leaders is that they stand in the place of God. They are God's representatives on earth speaking to the world about eternal realities. The discovery that a few of these leaders have been using their position of privilege to abuse children will be distressing in the extreme and they would rather not listen.

But hiding the truth, or hiding from the truth, is not a responsible option for Christians. If it is true that some church leaders have committed crimes against children, then this must be brought into the open. Jesus said of his followers, "You will know the truth and the truth will make you free" (John 8:32). In this spirit we begin our search for the truth.

1. Losing Our Innocence

Nothing is covered up that will not be uncovered,
and nothing secret that will not become known
(Jesus – Matt. 10:26)

The church has a problem. As an organization it has always set itself high moral standards and assumes that its members will adhere to these patterns of behaviour. In its own self-image it regards itself as the conscience of society, the guardian of morality, the community standard-bearer for ethical behaviour.

But suppose we were to uncover a particular form of immoral or criminal behaviour in which the leadership of the church is found to be a guilty party with a disproportionately high rate of offending: what would this do to the credibility of the church?

These are questions the church is now facing in many countries of the world. During the past decade there has been a depressingly long litany of clergy and Christian lay workers who have been arrested and convicted for sexual abuse. This has revealed an immoral underside to the church which most people would never have believed was possible. Terrible though this is, it has been compounded by the subterfuge and denial with which the church has tried to conceal the truth about the criminal actions of its people. These two acts of sexual abuse and denial are constantly in the media and have revealed what has been, and in some places still is, the hidden shame of the church.

The crime we are considering in this book is the deliberate sexual abuse of children. It is a criminal activity which, until recent times, has been covered over by a society which did not have the courage to face it. The implications of widespread abuse are too unpleasant for most people to contemplate. Consequently, the whole area of child sexual abuse has been surrounded by a culture of silence and denial in the community.

If we turn the clock back just a few years, the origins of this blindness can be partly understood through a personal experience of mine.

An early experience

Forty years ago I had just left seminary as a young pastor and entered my first church. It was typical of the post-war suburban clutter: a large housing estate with more children than adults and a host of social problems. We ran several clubs and programmes for children, and in the days before computers and television there was no problem rounding up a few hundred bored youngsters after school or during the school holidays.

My first nightmare came when two parents arrived to report that a young man who was one of the leaders in the boys' club had molested their children. Their evidence seemed fairly reliable so I assured them that the church would act promptly. I called an emergency meeting of the three senior elders of the church and placed the matter before them.

It was decided that immediate action was required, so while two elders remained in the church in prayer, the third elder and I went to the home of the young man who had been accused of the abuse. We told him that accusations had been made about his behaviour with young boys and we were there to seek the truth. He tried to explain what had happened, his mother became rather agitated, and within 15 minutes we were back on the street having been told that they would not be coming back to church and we could get someone else to run the boys' club.

When we returned to the church we felt elated, believing that somehow we had found a satisfactory solution to a difficult problem. It was now just a matter of meeting with the parents who had laid the complaints to tell them what had been done and the whole matter would be quickly forgotten. The church could then move on to more serious issues!

Seen in retrospect, it was a rather shameful event but it was typical of those times and, until quite recently, similar scenes would be played out in almost every church around the world.

If we analyze this simple situation in the light of our present knowledge, we see that the first and greatest mistake of those past days was to ignore the effect on the children who were abused. When the alleged abuse took place in our church, we did not try to determine the extent of it, nor did we consider its immediate or long-term effect on the lives of the abused boys. The community had no specialist services available to counsel children who had been abused and both the parents and the church elders took the pragmatic attitude that children were resilient, would soon forget the whole affair and no permanent damage would have been done. This was the conventional wisdom of the time.

Today we know it is not so simple. The aftermath of abuse on a child is rarely, if ever, forgotten. Feelings of guilt and/or shame keep recurring throughout life, and although there are resilient children who seem able to rise above the effects of child sex abuse many others continue to live with the memory of the abuse, which affects their behaviour and moods throughout their life. In some cases, the pain is so great that it will lead to suicide or other forms of self-destruction.

Protecting the church

The second error of the past was to give priority to the institution of the church ahead of the wellbeing of the children in its care. In this, as in every similar situation, the consensus of church leaders was very clear: "This will be bad for the church if it becomes public." The elders were good men. They were respected members of the community, each successful in his chosen career. So far as anyone knew, the elders themselves had not committed any great sin during their lives and they seemingly lived in happy and secure families.

The elders were passionate about "their" church. Between them they had substantially financed the original building and to them it was of paramount importance that the church should grow and become a significant force for good in the community.

When the alleged abuser threatened the good name of the church, the elders immediately closed ranks to find a way to stop this story becoming public knowledge. The resignation of the young man was considered a victory and the best possible solution to a potentially harmful problem. The parents would be certain not to tell anyone, the whole episode would be surrounded by silence, and it would be business as usual for the church.

In fact, as we now know, our action solved nothing. If the young man had indeed attempted to abuse some children, he needed help, not accusation. If he had actually abused a child, it was a criminal action. And worst of all, if he turned out to be a serial paedophile, there was the virtual certainty that he would continue to abuse a rather large number of other boys before he was caught again and he would probably be more careful to avoid detection. Our actions had simply ensured that this would now become a greater problem for some other group of people. But for the elders of the church in those days, this was not even considered. The real task they faced was to move the problem away from our own doorstep.

The church was not alone in its self-deception. It was following the common practice of society. Identical things were happening in schools, Boy Scouts, YMCAs, charities and other youth institutions. The behaviour of the authorities in these schools and organizations was always the same: the alleged offence was regarded as unfortunate but not serious enough to report to the police and, in any case, the good name of the group would be harmed by public scandal so it was much better to sweep the problem under the carpet. Leaders would argue that the cause was greater than the man, which was an escapist way of saying "let someone else have the problem".

Our ignorance of paedophilia was enormous. The word itself was never heard in the media or in conversation and few would have understood its meaning if they heard it. Society did not want to know there were such people threatening their children.

A typical story

We have travelled a long and painful journey in these past twenty years. Secrets about child abuse, which had been kept from the public for many years, have begun to come into the open. Adults who have suffered a life-time of painful memories have found the courage to accuse publicly prominent persons who had abused them as children. Too often the church has been an unwilling and unhappy defendant in these media and legal trials. Even with all these revelations, it is possible that what we see now is just the tip of a dangerous iceberg.

In 1996, the editor of a well-known magazine interviewed me about a book I had written on the sexual abuse of children. I was a little surprised that such a senior person would conduct the interview himself. He asked perceptive and well-researched questions but after a while it was apparent that his concentration was beginning to wander. Finally, he broke down in tears. Apologising for his "lack of professionalism", he began to unfold his own horror story of childhood abuse.

He had been a quiet and rather lonely young boy whose parents were active in the church. The parish priest enjoyed a close friendship with the family and showed special interest in the young boy. Slowly the priest won his confidence and eventually began to sexually abuse him in the privacy of the church vestry.

Shocked at what was happening, the boy tried to tell his mother a small part of what the priest had done. She promptly scolded him and told him never again to tell these terrible lies about the priest. With no friend to turn to, the boy suffered continual and increasing exploitation for the next few years until the priest moved on to another parish.

These events had taken place more than forty years earlier but they still had power to bring suffering to this adult editor. He said that he seldom went to bed at night without the remembrance of those terrible childhood years. The priest had eventually become a prominent leader in the church but had died before the editor could find the courage to confront him.

This is a typical story. Those who work with sexually abused children have heard almost identical stories from the memories of dozens of abused children and adults: the slow and careful cultivation of the child's trust while simultaneously winning the confidence of the parents. It is the hunter seeking the prey. It is predatory and it is destructive.

And, as we shall see, too much of this behaviour is found in the church.

2. What Is Happening to the Church?

God has been betrayed by his own kind
(comment by a survivor of clergy abuse)

In 1997 a Sydney-based author, Deborah Coddington, sought to bring the issue of child abuse into the public arena by publishing *The Australian Paedophile and Sex Offender Index*. She took information from the public domain and listed the names of more than 600 Australians who had received recent convictions for child sex abuse by Australian courts. In her introduction she wrote about the lengths to which some will go in order to have access to children. She noted that abusers become leaders of scout groups, kindergarten teachers or priests.

"In compiling this book," she said, "I was astonished by the number of clergy-related offenders – nearly 15 percent of the events fall into this category. Yet I doubt 15 percent of the professional workers in Australia are clergy so why a number disproportionately high?... What better disguise for a paedophile or rapist than the church, the most trusted, revered and respected institution in many people's lives."[1]

This is the spectre that is rising to haunt the church: the fear that, while the church preaches respect and compassion for children, it could possibly be a refuge centre for a disproportionate number of child sex abusers.

Until recently, all statistics on child sex abuse have been notoriously vague and speculative. They remain unsatisfactory, but the situation has certainly improved as academics and the media both begin to give the investigation of child abuse more serious attention. We are still unable to provide accurate answers to questions about the frequency of child sexual abuse in the churches. But even a quick survey of some major developments around the world in the past decade will indicate the seriousness of what is happening and will lead to the conclusion that the issue has already become a crisis for some churches.

Australia

We begin by looking at Australia, where Coddington and others have helped to make the sexual abuse of children a highly publicized issue. Coddington's book itself provides fairly depressing evidence about clerical participation in child sex abuse. Of the cases examined, 67 convictions were recorded against clergy or church-related persons. Most came from the two largest church institutions, with 60 percent of the total offenders being employed by the Catholic church and 15 percent by the Church of England (Episcopalian). The rest were mostly from fringe sects, with three cases from the mainline Protestant denominations. More than half of all the convictions involved active priests or pastors. Of the rest, teachers in church schools predominated.

Australia has become very conscious of the child sex abuse issue following a royal commission into police corruption in New South Wales in 1996. The commission exposed many public figures as secret paedophiles including politicians, a former mayor of Woolongong, radio personalities and school headmasters. The report included a special condemnation of the way paedophiles, both priest and laymen, were using the cover of the church to abuse children, especially through the teaching orders of private schools and in particular those run by the Christian Brothers.

The Catholic archdiocese of Melbourne has paid or offered to pay several million dollars in compensation to 80 victims of sexual abuse by 21 priests.

Research by two professors at Adelaide's University of South Australia in 1995 showed that almost 50 percent of child molesters in Australian jails claim to have been abused as children by priests or brothers.[2]

New Zealand

In 1996, Coddington published a paedophile and sex offender index for New Zealand with a list of offenders taken from the public domain. The book listed 570 cases of child sex abuse dating from 1990. The number of clergy and church-related offenders was lower than in Australia, less than 4 percent of the total.[3]

Within the total of 22 cases there were two Catholic priests, two Catholic brothers and four pastors of evangelical churches. The rest were laity, mostly leaders of church youth groups.

The church in New Zealand has not faced many child sex abuse cases involving clergy. Media attention has focused more on fringe cult groups such as the Centrepoint Community where the abuse of children was an accepted practice.

United Kingdom

In the six years 1995-2000, 26 priests were convicted of child sex abuse in England and Wales. The Welsh cases received wide publicity because of their seriousness. In October 2000 Fr Joseph Jordan was jailed for eight years for indecent assaults on young boys, possessing computer pornography and attempting to pervert the course of justice. The archbishop of Cardiff had ordained the priest in apparent contravention of church rules after he received, but ignored, warnings from another bishop who had expressed concern at Jordan's behaviour. In 1998, the archbishop's former press officer received sentences totalling eight years for rape and indecent assault.

A BBC documentary gave prominence to the issue and was critical of the passive role of the archbishop whose procedures were alleged to be so lax that they enabled these abuses to take place.

In response to these events, the Catholic bishops of England and Wales drew up new guidelines in 1994 to help the church deal with abuse cases. In 1996, a working party of bishops issued a public report which said that the church must move from its "culture of disbelief" about the "profound and frightening" effects of child sex abuse to one of more openness and honesty.[4]

In September 2000, the church announced it was introducing new measures to deal with priests who abuse children and a commission brought its report to the church in April 2001. It proposed the establishment of a national database for priests and a national child protection unit with representatives in every parish. The police will be asked to run checks on all clergy, staff and volunteers working for the church.

Ireland

The Irish Catholic church, working through its religious orders, was in charge of the country's industrial schools in the middle of the 20th century. During that time there was a pervasive pattern of child sex abuse in the schools which has now resulted in numerous claims against the church. It is estimated that from 1930 to 1969 about 20,000 children passed through the industrial and reformatory schools. Allegations of systematic abuse began to surface a few years ago and have since become a flood.

A Dublin school administered by the Christian Brothers is at the centre of the probe. It was closed in 1969 but a number of former pupils have laid complaints, making serious allegations of abuse while they were at the school. At least fifty former and serving members of the Christian Brothers Order are being investigated following complaints made against them.

In November 2000, Irish religious orders agreed in principle to participate in a compensation scheme for people who suffered abuse while in residential care as children, setting aside a sum of £100 million. This is in addition to other sums that have been paid in settlement of private cases brought against the church.

The government commission which is investigating the cases (the Laffoy Commission to Inquire into Child Abuse) received requests from about a thousand alleged victims to be represented at the hearings. In addition there have been 750 individuals initiating high court action. In November 2000 the church accepted its responsibility to pay a part of the £100 million which it is thought will be needed for compensation to the victims.[5]

In 1999, Prime Minister Bertie Ahern made an unprecedented apology for the country's failure to intervene and protect the children: "Too many of our children were denied love, care, security," he said.[6]

The Christian Brothers took out half-page advertisements in newspapers to apologise to the people of Ireland for their actions

Continental Europe

Cardinal Louis-Marie Bille of Lyon stated that by the year 2001 thirty French priests had been convicted of paedophilia and a further 18 priest are under investigation. Abbot Jean-Lucien Maunel was sentenced to ten years imprisonment in January of that year for raping and sexually abusing three boys.

In October 2000 a French court sentenced Rene Bisset, a former abbot of Caen and Mondeville, to 18 years' imprisonment for raping and abusing eleven young boys; the priest admitted the offences. Subsequently, a French magistrate initiated an investigation into Bisset's superior, Bishop Pierre Pican of Bayeaux, who is said to have known about Bisset's actions at least two years before his arrest, but since it was revealed in the confessional Bishop Pican would not pass on the information to the authorities.[7]

In **Austria**, allegations of child sex abuse against Cardinal Hans Groer led to a crisis of faith for many Catholics. Thousands of Austrian church members are said to have renounced their faith since allegations against the cardinal by five of his former pupils first surfaced in March 1995. After the accusations, Cardinal Groer resigned from his position as head of the church in Austria. However, the church declined to investigate the allegations and a protest group known as "We Are the Church" was launched. The group called for a referendum on whether to investigate the case but this was ignored. Estimates of those who left the church as a result of this conflict number as high as half a million.

In March 1998, five Austrian bishops said they thought the allegations against Cardinal Groer were true "in essence". Finally, the pope ordered an internal inquiry to try and restore the status of the church in Austria.

In April 1998, Groer was ordered to give up his duties and go into exile which is understood to be an indication that the investigation had found against him.

Child sex abuse has a high profile in **Belgium** since the Dutroux arrest in 1996 revealed a terrible story of abuse and the murder of a number of children by a Belgian paedophile.

In a case of child abuse two years later, the priest who admitted the crime was given a six-year jail sentence but the court also required the Belgian Cardinal Danneels to pay damages to a boy who had been molested at the age of 12 years. The court ruled that since the priest was under the authority of the cardinal it was the latter's responsibility to accept the consequences of the crime.

Canada

In January 1998 the federal government issued a formal apology for its residential school system which had been administered by religious groups and aimed at assimilating Native American children into Canadian society.

Soon after this announcement the law-suits began to be submitted and are still arriving at the rate of twenty new cases every day. By June 2000 the number of individuals suing the federal government had reached 5900 and it is esti-mated that the final number will be as many as 15,000. To date only 300 cases have been settled.

In February 2001, the federal government announced a $2 billion grant to cover the cost of residential school law-suits. Churches have been asked to contribute to the cost as well. The Anglican church will be expected to raise $95.6 million over the next 10-15 years.

The abuse cases took place while the churches were administering the schools, but because of the large number of claims the federal government is working with the churches to find a financial solution.

There has been considerable pressure on the churches. In October 2000 the Anglican diocese of Cariboo in Western Canada voted to disband within twelve months. The church is faced with the prospect of bankruptcy emerging from com-pensation claims that were ordered for numerous cases of child abuse. The abuse had occurred some years previously at the Anglican St George's School in Lytton, 150 kilometres north-east of Vancouver.

The *Ottawa Sun* newspaper, which has carried out inves-tigations into child sex abuse within the Catholic church, has identified 32 priests who had either been charged or convicted of sex crimes since the mid-1980s.

In Ottawa itself, the Catholic church faces a number of civil suits, with 350 male victims said to have been abused by church leaders. A $24 million fund has been established to meet these claims.

In the province of Newfoundland there have been several cases against the Christian Brothers who operate an orphanage. In one case in Ontario, 19 Christian Brothers were convicted of child abuse at a school.

In another high profile case, Canadian Bishop Hubert O'Connor was found guilty of rape and indecent assault during the time he was principal of a Native residential school in Williams Lake thirty years previously. He was convicted and sentenced to two-and-a-half years' imprisonment but was acquitted later on the indecent assault charge, and the rape charge was dropped after the accuser and the police agreed to hold a "healing circle" instead. The decision to drop the charges, and the fact that the bishop has not admitted to the sexual abuse, has angered First Nation people.

United States

It is difficult to know where to start when describing the complex situation in the United States of America. No other country has experienced as much controversy over wayward priests and pastors as the USA. Child sex abuse by Christian clergy and laity has seldom been out of the news and has undoubtedly affected the public perception of the church and its ministry.

Many non-governmental organizations have been established to monitor developments and to give support to survivors (the term "survivors" is used to describe those who have been abused as children and who have found some way to go on living, although this was achieved with great difficulty in many cases). Web sites offer specialized help to survivors who have been abused by clergy from the Orthodox, Catholic, Anglican, Mormon and Protestant churches or one of many other religious or Christian groups.

One of the survivor groups in America, SNAP (Survivors Network of those Abused by Priests), estimates that in the Catholic church alone about a thousand paedophile priests have been identified in the past 15 years. This represents 2 percent of the 49-50,000 Catholic priests in America. Tom Economus, president of another group supporting survivors of clergy abuse (Linkup), estimates that the Catholic church has paid $1 billion ($1,000,000,000) in sexual abuse lawsuits, attorney fees and settlements and this has been endorsed by the *National Catholic Reporter*. Writing in 1999, Economus based these figures on a review of 1400 court cases plus information from insurance companies and abuse victims.

Some writers have suggested that out-of-court settlements and other quiet payments would make the $1 billion estimate a conservative figure. But by whatever standard of measurement, the economic cost to the Catholic church in America is considerable. So much so that some dioceses, including Chicago and Santa Fe, have been on the verge of bankruptcy.

A record sum was paid when the wealthy Dallas diocese was ordered to turn over $120 million in damages for the actions of a single priest. The damages were awarded to ten former altar boys who had been abused a total of 1350 times by Fr Rudolph Kos between 1981 and 1992, plus damages to the family of another boy who had committed suicide after years of abuse. In July 1998, the diocese made a payment of $31 million to the former altar boys.

The jury decision was aimed not only at the priest but also at the diocese. They found the diocese guilty of gross negligence, malice, conspiracy and fraud in failing to stop Kos abusing the children and in trying later to cover up evidence of his actions.

Richard Sipe, an ordained Catholic priest now married and living in retirement in Maryland, has written three influential books on the child sex abuse crisis in the Catholic church of America. His research led him to conclude that only 50 percent of American priests practise celibacy and very few achieve it completely. Since 1960, 20,000 priests have left active priesthood in the USA, the majority to marry. At any one time, Sipe claims, 20 percent of priests in good standing are involved in sexual relationships with women and another 8 percent are experimenting sexually.[8]

The situation in the diocese of Santa Rosa in California is a recent case that illustrates the extent to which widespread child abuse by clergy has affected the church. A new bishop was appointed to the diocese in August 1999 to try and clean up what the *San Francisco Chronicle* called "a diocese torn by charges of child molestation, embezzlement and extortion, and clergy sex scandals".[9]

The previous bishop of the diocese, Patrick Ziemann, resigned in July after one of his own clergy filed a lawsuit accusing him of sexual abuse. The priest accuser was himself alleged to have stolen money from a local parish. The bishop admitted that he had a sexual relationship but said it was consensual. During the years when Bishop Ziemann was head of the diocese, five diocesan priests were accused of child molestation. One is in a state prison, another killed himself and a third fled to Mexico.

According to the Newhouse news service every one of the 188 dioceses in the United States has faced a child abuse case against its employees.

Within mainline Protestant and Orthodox churches in America, there have also been a number of major sex scandals but these have usually been for sexual harassment rather than child sex abuse. Prominent television evangelists such as Jimmy Swaggart and Jim Bakker were among the church leaders accused of sexual impropriety.

Into all the world

The best-documented cases of child sex abuse are in Western countries and these continue to make headlines in the news.

Less visible, but equally damaging to the mission of the church, is the paedophile activity of some missionaries and church workers who have been posted to overseas countries where they use their position of influence to exploit local children.

Covenant House in New York was always held up as a model programme for helping street children. In the late 1980s, rumours of child abuse in the organization led to the resignation of its charismatic director, Father Bruce Ritter. He left under a cloud of suspicion and refused to undergo counselling. Eventually, he was transferred to a rural parish in remote Allepy, Kerala, India.

While still at Covenant House, Ritter helped found a sister programme in Central America called Casa Allianza. Early in 1990, its director was dismissed when it was found that he had abused young boys. The new director, Bruce Harris, wasted no time in cleaning up the organization. He found lax rules and lack of accountability which made it easy for staff to sexually abuse children. Within four months he had fired at least six employees, with four of them charged with molesting children. His actions were later confirmed as justifiable by Kroll Associates, a firm of private investigators.

In Africa and Asia there have been numerous accusations against foreigners working in orphanages and children's programmes. From 1990 to 1998 I was working in Asia with ECPAT (the international group which deals with child prostitution, child pornography and trafficking in children). The office regularly received reports of foreigners who were suspected of sexually abusing children. These are a few examples of accusations against Christian groups from the files of those years:

1. Two separate children's Christian charities were set up in the chaos of post-war Cambodia, one established by an American, another by a European. Both men were found to be bribing officials to send children overseas for adoption and both were reported to be abusing children. No action was taken by government authorities.
2. An Australian priest built a large home near the river in Pagsanjan, Philippines, which was used for regular boys' parties at which many foreign paedophiles were present.

The priest was later arrested and imprisoned for child sex abuse.

3. An Irish churchman studying for the priesthood was expelled from seminary after being found to be sexually abusing minors. When last seen he was trying to set up a children's orphanage in a rural region of Asia.

4. A clergyman from Europe left his parish under a cloud of suspicion following accusations he had abused children. He moved to a remote area in South-East Asia where he established a programme to rehabilitate young boys who had worked in bars.

5. Members of the Mormon church opened a large orphanage in Bangkok for street children. It was also used as a hotel by American paedophiles. The Thai authorities closed the orphanage and arrested the three leaders who each served a brief jail term.

These are a few of many accounts received over a period of seven years. In most cases, the programmes initiated by the alleged abuser were the action of an individual who was using the church to give credibility to his crime.

Within the mainstream missionary movement there have also been accusations against established mission programmes and individual missionaries. It is a situation which mission boards find hard to handle and it seems likely that most of the accusations have been ignored because of the inability of the mission boards to deal adequately with the case. Of the three situations with which I am familiar, the information has been sent to the mission headquarters but the complexity of securing evidence or working in a foreign culture proved too daunting for the church and the accusations were not properly investigated. The isolation of the missionaries has protected them from an examination of their actions.

Operating in the relative anonymity of a developing country, the child sex abuser has had many advantages. The disadvantaged and sometime illiterate children of the poor are easy targets for an abuser. The abuser can do what he wishes with children and then buy their silence, or the connivance of the parents, with a small sum of money or a cheap gift.

Along the coastal regions of Sri Lanka, Thailand and the Philippines, local social workers can point to houses of foreign paedophiles, usually behind tall fences, which are open to regular visits by young boys or girls. In rural areas where the local people are struggling for survival, it is not uncommon for parents to encourage their children to tout for business among the paedophile community as a means of securing money for the family.

In the unlikely event that an accusation is brought against an abuser it has been, at least until recently, a common and simple matter to bribe the underpaid police to overlook the case.

Throughout the history of the church, missionaries have travelled to remote areas in the furthest corners of the world, beyond the reach of television interviewers or investigative reporters. In their passion to reach all the lost tribes they have endured great hardship and worked in inhospitable regions where survival is a daily gamble for the communities. A small percentage of these missionaries have exploited the people in their care for their own sexual gratification.

In August 2000, after speaking at a convention in Brisbane, Australia, I was approached by a group of Aboriginals who gave graphic accounts of the way some missionaries had abused Aboriginal children. Children had been removed from their parents to live with missionary families, where they were expected to meet all the demands of their benefactors. Their sad stories reflected and confirmed the accounts told to the government royal commission which investigated paedophile behaviour in Australia.

The Christian missionary sex abuser has built-in protection. In most countries of Asia and Africa and among tribal communities, the holy man is venerated and respected. To speak against such a person who has dedicated himself to the service of God is psychologically impossible for many local people. If a missionary child abuser is to be brought to justice, it will have to be done without the full cooperation of local people. The best solution for this problem is to deal with the issue in advance, at the point of selection of missionaries, rather than trying to sort out problems of sexual abuse once the abuser is living and working in the mission field.

There is anecdotal evidence of child sex abuse in Asian, Latin American, Pacific and African churches but these have rarely become public. The control over women and children in some of these situations is thought to be the reason these crimes are hidden from public attention.

This book concentrates on Christianity and the churches, but it should be noted that both Buddhism and Hinduism are facing similar problems, with their religious leaders being publicly accused of abuse against women or children. Among the celibate orders of Buddhism there is a common perception that monks regularly develop a sexual relationship with one of their young novices.

The public prosecution of high-profile monks for sexual activities is a new development that has brought the matter to the public in south-east Asia. In November 2000, the arrest and conviction of prominent monk Phra Khru raised wide-ranging debate in Thai newspapers about the behaviour of wayward monks.

Hinduism is not exempt. The sale of young girls into temple prostitution *(devadasi)* has a long history and still exists in many parts of India even though it is officially against the law. More recently the fringe groups within Hinduism have been centres of dispute. Renowned guru Sai Baba has drawn tens of thousands of followers from around the world, but stories of his sexual exploitation of young boys have been constantly reported. A document called *The Findings* was published in 2000 by two of his former devotees. Much of their report deals with testimonies of sexual harassment and sexual abuse. Also in 2000 the Hindu movement Hare Krishna has been forced to close its schools in the United States after forty former students brought a $400 million law suit against the sect claiming abuse over two decades.

Questions for the churches

The accounts of child sex abuse cases recorded in this chapter are not intended to be comprehensive. They are simply a collection of some of the high-profile stories about churches and child sex abuse compiled from the world's media over the past five years. But such a collection does show that the public is now aware that there is a serious problem in the church. They will expect some reasonable response from church authorities.

Analyzing these many reports we are left with several questions:

- A number of the sex abuse cases brought against the clergy are in relation to crimes which were committed twenty, thirty or even more years previously. Clearly, there must have been significant social pressure in the past which prevented these matters coming to public attention and it is distressing to realize that victims have had to carry this heavy silence for so many years. Questions will inevitably be raised about the reliability of memory in analyzing an event that took place up to forty years previously. But it is indicative of the traumatic impact of such abuse that many survivors have been able to recapture the details of the abuse so long after it occurred.

- This leads to the central question of credibility. How can so many religious leaders have allowed themselves to act in such an immoral and criminal fashion towards those who trusted them? People look to their religious leaders to lead honest and responsible lives and in most respects this has happened. It is extremely rare to hear of any religious leaders convicted of murder or drug dealing or any crime of this nature. Why then a blockage on the sexual abuse of children, a crime which some would argue is one of the least acceptable of all?

- In most countries where clergy abuse has taken place, a disproportionate number of high-profile cases have involved clergy of the Catholic church. Legal action has been taken against quite large numbers of priests and teaching brothers and there have been recent public accusations against at least ten bishops and two cardinals. In the search for reasons for this imbalance, many commentators have spoken of the influence of mandatory celibacy as being a significant factor behind clergy abuse. Former priest Richard Sipe puts this perception quite bluntly: "The scandal of priestly sexual abuse of minors, although real and significant of itself, is primarily a symptom of an essentially flawed celibate/sexual system of ecclesiastical power."[10]

- In almost all the cases of clergy abuse listed above, there has been widespread community reaction to the way the church has handled accusations against its clergy. Those within the life of the church know how much the church exists as a self-sufficient sub-culture with its own rules and ways of operating. In much of its decision-making, the church operates like a secret society with its own independent ways of reaching decisions. This is largely an historical inheritance, but it is out of step with the move within modern society for democratic decision-making and an open society.

- When the church is suddenly thrown into a public crisis situation that demands damage control, it appears to have no experience to fall back on, and has handled many of the clergy sex cases with a naivety that has angered both victims and the wider community. It has given rise to public perception that the church cares more about preserving its own organization than it does about the children who have been abused.

- Central to the problem facing the church is its theological understanding of human behaviour. Confession and the forgiveness of sin play a central role in Christian faith. The way these two practices operate is being challenged by the rise of child sex abuse within the church.

Has the church, then, been too lax in its requirements for those who are ordained to be priests or pastors? The fact that so many child sex abusers have made it through the selection and training system of the church and become missionaries, teachers or clergy reflects badly on church protocols and procedures. Change is required.

Some of these questions will be explored in more detail in later chapters.

The gender issue

This summary of child sex abusers has sometimes used gender-specific words (he and him) to describe the generic class of child sex abusers. This may seem a little unfair because it is now recognized that there are female paedophiles as well as male. But the truth is that the number of women sexually abusing children is exceedingly small and all the high-profile cases recorded above are those of male abusers.

The role of women has sometimes been as accessories to the crimes of child sex abuse in both child prostitution and child pornography. Women have sold their children to sex slavery in poor countries, or been the Mama-san of a children's brothel, or collaborated in the production of child pornography. But the actual abusers and the creators of the demand for children are almost always male.

NOTES

[1] Deborah Coddington, *The Australian Paedophile and Sex Offender Index,* Mount View Trust, 1997.
[2] AFP News, July 95.
[3] Deborah Coddington, *The 1996 Paedophile and Sex Offender Index*, Mount View Trust, 1996.
[4] *The Times*, 4 Sept. 1996.
[5] *Irish Times*, 23 Nov. 2000.
[6] *Irish Times*, 11 May 1999.
[7] Reuters 3 Jan. 2000.
[8] Richard Sipe, *Sex, Priests and Power*, London, Cassell, 1995.
[9] 14 Aug. 1999.
[10] Sipe, *op. cit.*, p.4.

3. Christianity – Children – Sex

Child sex abuse by church leaders challenges the church to reassess its theological beliefs in order to see whether there are some systems which need to be revised or developed. Three which are of particular importance in this area are the Christian understanding of the place of children in society, the way we use confession and forgiveness in the church, and the broad question of sexual relations versus no sexual relations (celibacy).

A theology of the child

Christian beliefs were founded and formed in a tribal era. By the time of Jesus, some tribes had moved from being nomadic to a more settled life-style. Small towns and villages were built around trade routes, religious centres or areas of arable land, but most communities remained tribal-based. From time to time tribes would combine to defend their own self-interest from invaders but there was little sense of nationhood as it is understood today.

In this context, children played a critical role. They were the tribe's best hope for future defence and they provided social security for members of the family as they grew older. Not surprisingly, the bearing and rearing of children was an essential part of a tribe's life-style and dominated the thoughts and attention of the people.

Was Sarah barren? This was a shame and a disgrace. Let her husband take a slave woman to bear children. Did David's son die in an accident? Then let the whole tribe go into mourning. At the most basic level of survival, the child was the centre of importance for the whole community. Without many children the tribe had no future.

The Old Testament records show that being childless was thought to be a great tragedy and a punishment from God. The strongest curse Isaiah could invoke upon Babylon was that its women would become barren. A family without children was a disaster for the tribe.

Conversely, it was seen as the blessing of God when a family had many children, especially if they were sons. In the days before women went to war, the sons would be the first line of defence against a marauding tribe.

> Sons are indeed a heritage from the Lord,
> the fruit of the womb a reward.
> Like arrows in the hand of a warrior
> are the sons of one's youth.
> Happy is the man who has his quiver full of them.
> He shall not be put to shame
> When he speaks with the enemies in the gate.
> (Ps. 127:3-5)

But there was a qualification. It was not enough to bear children, they must also conform to tribal norms and values. The mother looked after the domestic side of the family while the father took responsibility for training his sons in the ways of warfare and teaching them the religious basis from which the tribe developed its cohesion and strength.

> Training the child meant discipline.
> "Hear, my child, your father's instructions,
> and do not reject your mother's teaching."
> (Prov. 1:8)

> "A wise child loves discipline."
> (Prov. 13:1)

The child was never seen as an isolated individual but as a part of the community. A major function in life for every member of the tribe was to conform to the common values and thus ensure the survival of the clan. Punishment was meted out as a means to ensure conformity and dependence, though there are several examples in history of it causing some children to rebel and leave their tribe.

In biblical times before property or legal rights were established, most ownership was built on traditional assumptions rather than on law. It was customary to assume that children were "owned" by the parents. Children could be given away or sold by the father; children were a property, a chattel of the family, until they had passed through the rites of passage which made them full members of the tribe. Even then, strict tribal hierarchy made them subservient to tribal elders.

The attitude of the church towards children during the first period of the Christian era continued to be based on tribal survival and led to four basic beliefs:
– a family without children is bad;
– having many children (especially sons) is good;
– children should be disciplined through punishment;
– children are the property of their parents.

The position of children today

Society has changed dramatically in the last century and with these changes many of the assumptions on which tribal community was built have lost their significance. In a welfare state, a large family with many children is no longer needed as a form of social security. And with the growing sophistication of surveillance, law enforcement, conflict and warfare, the security of a household or community is not dependent on large families for its defence and protection.

Many other factors such as improved health care, increased longevity, working parents and modern city life-styles have contributed to a sharp decline in the size of families in almost all economically developed countries. Children are no longer a requirement for living a full and happy life, and increasing numbers of young people are aware that they can survive quite well in life without being parents.

The other tribal imperatives of stern discipline towards, and ownership of, children are also fast disappearing. Faced with a wide range of choices, the modern young person who is subjected to old-fashioned discipline is likely to walk away from the family and set up an independent life, or even lodge a cruelty case with the authorities. Such independence, obviously, was not possible for most young people in biblical times.

There are exceptions in the modern era, even in developed countries. Cult religious groups, which regard themselves as being constantly persecuted by the wider community, or groups of foreign migrants trying to retain their identity as a minority community in a much larger population, still continue to follow Old Testament patterns as a form of preservation. They are more inclined to have large families and to see discipline and the use of severe punishment as key factors in ensuring the survival of their community.

If the traditional biblical understanding of children is no longer relevant for the majority of people, where do we look for guidance and inspiration?

It has become customary in the church today to speak of the need for a return to "family values", but it is not clear what the church means by this. If it means mum and dad and a large number of children held together by a strict discipline standing around the piano singing hymns, then it will almost certainly fail – and deservedly so. The world has moved into new and more creative forms of elective tribalism, and survival is no longer dependent on having large families of disciplined warriors. In the new global society, the old norms of family life can no longer determine our life-style.

The life-style of the Western world in particular is creating a new understanding of the role of children and the church is threatened with the likelihood of being left irrelevant on the margins of society unless it can understand these changes and contribute to them in a more positive manner.

The new direction for children in society was articulated in some detail in September 1990 when the nations of the world signed, and subsequently ratified, the United Nations Convention on the Rights of the Child. The convention received wider and faster endorsement by nations than any previous UN document and is now universally accepted. What is more, the convention includes a reporting mechanism which ensures that the values and ideals included in the document will eventually be the basis on which all countries of the world formulate their laws and treat their children.

The understanding of children inherent in the convention represents a quantum leap from the traditional Jewish and Christian values that we have been teaching for years and which were the basis on which we built Western society. But the convention itself has hardly been noted by the church and is little known outside a small circle of child advocates.

Even to speak of children possessing rights is a foreign language for many Christians. The ideal child for many is still "the one who is seen and not heard", and most Christian parents will make their own unilateral decisions on what is right for their children. Some continue to quote the Old Testament:

> Those who spare the rod, hate their children
> but those who love them are diligent to discipline them.
> (Prov. 13:24)

This may be a comforting thought for some parents but a modern life-style makes such a viewpoint extremely difficult to realize. Many children spend more quality time in school with teachers and friends than they do at home; one or possibly both of the parents will be away from home for long hours; and the church, once the arbiter of behaviour, has little attraction for most young people. When you put these three factors together, the possibility of the family exerting the control over children that was exercised by earlier generations is quite remote. Today, much of the training to which children respond comes from their television sets and computers or from their peers and celebrity role models rather than from their parents.

The changed social context in which we live is already leaving many church leaders behind when it comes to the place and role of children. This is shown quite clearly in the responses made by some clergy in relation to allegations of child sex abuse. They attempt to minimize the significance of their action with throw-away lines. "It happens to all kids", or "it's just part of growing up, they'll get over it". Such comments can be read as simply justification for irresponsible adult behaviour and fail to recognize that the child has rights that must be observed.

The traditions of the past left adults free to make whatever judgments they chose in relation to their children and the only option for the child was obedience. But the days when adults were automatically right and a child was *just* a child have gone for ever. Children of today will increasingly be seen, heard and (usually) believed.

The Convention on the Rights of the Child turns the old concepts upside down. It asserts that there are independent and inalienable rights which the child possesses simply by being a child, and that these have priority over alternative rights which some parents or members of society might consider more appropriate. There are still many glitches in the implementation of this convention but the principle of children's rights, like the Declaration on Human Rights, is here to stay. It requires a thorough reassessment of our theological understanding of children and their place in society.

For example: Does this mean that the child has the right to participate in decisions that affect him or her? Note that we are asking whether the child has *the right*, and not has the child *the possibility*. This right is one of many enshrined in the convention but, apart from a few tentative experiments with this radical concept by some governments and youth programmes, it has largely been ignored and is, consequently, ineffective.

As presently structured the church will find it an even more difficult, if not impossible, step to give children the right to participate in decision-making processes which affect them. Almost all churches operate on a hierarchical system in which seniority gives added authority. The idea that children and young people have decision-making rights is the antithesis of traditional church views where rules are handed down from above. The design of most church buildings reflects this hierarchical view with the congregation seated in formal rows facing the clerical spokesperson for God. The people stand when told to, close their eyes when praying, and sit obediently and without question when they are told what the teaching of the church is. To reinforce this authority, the minister will often be standing in a defensive pulpit or on an elevated platform, six feet above argument. In the church, seniority, age and rank still have priority over youth.

Children of today do not understand this world. They are growing up in an atmosphere where it is appropriate to ask questions and where they are encouraged to seek answers for themselves. If the UN convention is universally implemented children will soon be demanding their own rights. New technologies have provided them with access to information and knowledge more extensive than their parents could ever know. Most parents are strangers in this new world and have little experience in knowing how to act appropriately. In the area of pornography, for example, many parents have become anxious and paranoid about the way their children use computers, but they are dependent on what others are telling them since they have little understanding of how the internet works. But they *do* understand that their authority is slowly being eroded by their own children, whose expertise in technology has already begun to challenge the parents' status in the family.

Whatever changes occur in the next decades, the concept of children's rights will have a central place in the new world and it will force us into fresh recognition of the importance of children. Viewing children in this new way has the potential to provide mechanisms that will protect children from those who would exploit them. This in turn will place knowledge and information at our fingertips and offer new ways of creating an international society in which all people can develop to their full potential in security and love. The church should welcome such a development. But first it has to understand it.

Confession and forgiveness

The confession of sin and the forgiveness of sin are central tenets of the Christian faith. In their regular order of worship almost all Christian churches include an act of public confession followed by the pronouncement of forgiveness. This is almost always a generalized act without reference to the specific sins of individuals in the congregation.

The early church practised a public confession that was more specific. Members were encouraged to stand up during

the church worship and make their confession to other wor-
shippers. The book of James encouraged members of the
young church to "confess your sins to one another and pray
for one another" (James 5:16)

Individual confessions in which Christians made their
confession to a priest did not enter into the usual practice of
the church until the late 6th century. It became increasingly
common and was made part of the doctrine of the Western
church at the Lateran council in 1215. The council initiated a
rule that active members of the church are required to make
a private or auricular confession at least once a year.

Strict rules governed the practice of the confessional
through which the confessor was constrained to keep
absolute secrecy. The code of canon law of the Catholic
church speaks about the seal of confession in these words.

> The sacramental seal is inviolable. Consequently the confessor
> must exercise all diligent care not to betray the penitent in any
> degree by word, sign or in any other way or for any excuse
> whatsoever. (c889)

According to the *New Catholic Encyclopaedia*,

> The law of the seal admits no excusation [sic]. No cause, how-
> ever great, whatever the circumstances will justify its violation.
> The seal is inviolable.

In practice this means that the priest may not ever refer to
the issue outside the confessional. He may not take up the
matter with the person concerned even if he has confessed to
being a serial paedophile. It is also considered to be a viola-
tion of the seal if the priest takes any action to make use of
the knowledge obtained in a confession.

The institution of private confession remains operative in
the Roman Catholic Church although its practice has
declined markedly in most countries. Where it still continues
in its original form it raises serious questions:
– Failure to report a crime is usually regarded as a criminal
offence in itself. In most countries the church practice of
confidential confession has been above this law but this

exemption is increasingly being questioned, especially when the confession is linked with forgiveness. How important is the practice of this kind of confession?

In some circumstances it gives the priest authority to protect persons who are guilty of a serious crime or to ignore the cry of the innocent. In these cases confession becomes a practice which must be seriously questioned.

- When a priest knows from the confessional that a man is a child sex abuser, he is forbidden to use that knowledge outside the confessional. But how is he able to stand aside and watch a confessed paedophile take children to his home without being compelled to act to protect the children?

Conflict between the church and civil law has surfaced in some child sex abuse accusations. In the French case of René Bisset, mentioned earlier, the failure of his bishop to report the crime of child sexual abuse could bring a prison sentence of up to three years.[1]

The bishop of Bisset had known that his priest was abusing children because it had been spoken of in the confessional, but under canon law he was unable to say anything to a third party. For Bisset, the situation seemed quite clear. He stated that he had made his confession and his confessors had pardoned him for his sins and told him "things will work out".

The forgiveness of sin is the action of God in Christ who knows the human heart. None of us are in a position to know the inner heart of a penitent; we can only hope that the confession of sin is genuine, will be followed by honest reparation, and the sinner will "go and sin no more". But it is not good enough to leave the abuser believing that his simple confession of a criminal act in secrecy (or even openly) can automatically bring forgiveness. The statement by Bisset that "his confessors had pardoned him for his sins" indicates the misunderstanding that surrounds the act of confession and forgiveness. The abuser must accept responsibility for his actions before any healing or any forgiveness can take place.

A similar misunderstanding is found in many churches. Recently, the leaders of a large Pentecostal church in New Zealand discovered that one of their youth ministers had been sexually abusing young children from the Sunday school. He was summoned to appear before the church elders who faced him with the clear evidence of his actions. The man broke down in tears and prayed for forgiveness. The elders and the pastor prayed over the man and pronounced that he was forgiven. The pastor then spoke to a number of people and told them that Brother X had sinned but that he had confessed his sin and was now pardoned. He told the congregation that the episode was closed and now they must "forgive and forget". Within a few weeks Brother X was caught abusing another child. He is now in prison.

The pressure on Christians to "forgive and forget" is quite common, but in practice it will often end up as a form of blackmail. It is especially insensitive to those who have been abused. They have been badly hurt psychologically by the abuse, they already feel a sense of shame from the experience, and now they are being coerced to show forgiveness to the abuser. Naturally they find that difficult and sometimes impossible merely on the basis of a few sentences of confession by their abuser. But if the victims decline to show forgiveness in these circumstances, they will be made to carry an additional sense of guilt in the eyes of the church. They will be seen as bad Christians because they couldn't forgive as they were commanded to do by Christ.

But there is no such thing as cheap grace.

Forgiveness is costly and must be earned.

If the church is to deal with child sex abuse in a more rational way, there needs to be a better understanding of the way child sex abusers operate. Paedophiles will say anything at all – they will repent in tears, walk across hot coals, anything to avoid facing the reality of what they are and what they are doing. They dwell in a fantasy world where they feel able to follow different rules to the rest of society and where they use specious arguments to justify their immoral behaviour.

To accept the repentance of such men on their verbal assurance and then to say that the church and the victim must "forgive and forget" shows a naivety about the way paedophiles think. It ignores the obsessional nature of child sex abuse and is insensitive to the permanent psychological damage abusers do to their victims.

Sex and celibacy

Thanks in part to the feminist revolution and the debate over women clergy, there have been dozens of excellent books written on the Christian understanding of sexuality in recent years. We do not have to repeat these important debates here, but the consensus which seems to have emerged is that our modern "Christian" views of sex owe more to the teaching of the church fathers than they do to the words and actions of Jesus.

In the gospels, there is very little record of Jesus speaking about human sexuality. His life and ministry was so completely focused on his mission to proclaim the salvation of God that we have to assume that sexual relationships were not a central issue for him.

While his teaching on sexuality was not extensive, the actions of Jesus spoke volumes about his attitude to basic human relationships. The recorded encounters he has with women and children are characterized by a total respect for the other person regardless of age or gender. In particular his meeting at the well with the woman of Samaria (John 4), his dealings with the prostitute who poured ointment on his feet (John 7:36f.) and his confrontation with accusers of the woman taken in adultery (John 8:1-11), show a sensitivity to women that must have been rare and unique for his time.

Three hundred years after the death of Christ, attitudes towards sexuality became increasingly dogmatic. Formative in this change was the group of men we call the church fathers. Among these patriarchs the influence of three men was of particular importance: Tertullian, a theologian of Carthage; Jerome, a learned Italian scholar; and Augustine of Hippo, whose books remain classics of devotion to this day.

The teaching they developed had profound influence on all subsequent Christian teaching of sexual ethics. The three men came from pagan backgrounds and each led an active sex life before being converted to Christianity. With the zeal of converts they taught an interpretation of Christianity which today would be considered misogynist but which has influenced the churches for centuries and still lingers on in many parts of the church. As commentators now agree, their views were developed from the prevailing Greek thinking rather than from either the Old or the New Testament.

Augustine, the greatest of the Latin fathers, struggled throughout his life to understand the conflict between the temporal and the spiritual. His monumental *City of God* is a series of 22 books that record this struggle and the final victory in which the church becomes triumphant. In his explanation of the origins of sin, Augustine went back to the story of Adam and Eve in the Old Testament and developed the doctrine of original sin. From that starting point he established a causal link between original sin and sexuality.

To Augustine, the act of intercourse was fundamentally disgusting and he referred to it as the uncontrolled lust of procreation. Jerome said it was "unclean" and Tertullian called it "shameful". Needless to say, there was nothing in the teaching of Jesus that would support these views.

While the first Christians seemed to have a positive view on the role of women in the church, the Latin fathers inverted this view to estrange women from any respectability. Take this extraordinary statement on women from Tertullian:

> Do you not know that you are each an Eve? The sentence of God on this sex of yours lives in this age: the guilt must of necessity live too. You are the devil's gateway; you are the unsealer of that forbidden tree; you are the first deserter of the divine law; you are she who persuaded him whom the devil was not valiant enough to attack. You so carelessly destroyed man, God's image. On account of your desert, even the Son of God had to die.[2]

The opinions of the church fathers steered the Western church to defining a direct connection between sexuality and sin and to developing the theory that marriage is acceptable for procreation purposes but celibacy is better. As this view became common, it laid the foundation for the practice of celibacy in the priesthood. Over the next centuries celibacy slowly gained ground, and by the Middle Ages it had become an absolute requirement for priests. This was reinforced in the 11th-century reforms of the church by Pope Gregory VII, who described the marriage of priests as "a crime of fornication".

The issue of mandatory celibacy for priests, however, was always surrounded by controversy. Even during the Gregorian reforms and the Lateran council of 1215 there was no consensus of opinion on the matter. In Nordic countries, strong opposition to priestly celibacy delayed its universal implementation for at least two centuries. Since many senior clergy and bishops had concubines there was always a strong lobby for lifting the restriction on marriage.

Throughout these years, the practice of celibacy was confined to the Western/Latin church and it remains one of the continuing differences between the Catholic church and Eastern rite churches. The Eastern churches always allowed priests and deacons to marry before ordination and remain married afterwards. Bishops were excluded from this practice and were normally selected from among the ranks of monks or unmarried priests. Eastern rite churches still preserve the tradition of a married clergy.

The late Patriarch Maximus Saigh claimed that the marriage laws of the Orthodox church meant that it did not have to face the same problems of paedophilia and sex scandals as the Catholic church. He wrote to the Vatican with this message: "With the freedom of choice (celibacy or marriage) we have to deplore fewer faults and admire more virtues."

The Protestant Reformation between the 14th and 17th centuries challenged many of the Augustinian doctrines of sexual morality. Most significantly, it did away with the subordination of marriage to celibacy. Luther himself had been an Augustinian monk but came to consider compulsory chastity to be positively damaging to the clergy.

He married a former nun and in a sermon in 1531 stated: "Under the papacy, marriage was thought to be inferior and all praise was heaped on the unmarried state into which almost everyone was forced." Most of the other leaders of the Reformation were priests and they agreed with Erasmus when he said that the church should turn concubines into wives.

Celibacy today

In today's world, the question of celibacy has assumed major proportions in relation to child sex abuse. Whenever there is a high-profile case involving a Catholic priest there is a public demand for reasons. Why is it that highly principled men of God can commit such inexplicable crimes against children? What is wrong with the church that such things should take place? In Europe and the United States, the discussion almost always raises the possibility of a linkage between the enforcement of priestly celibacy and child sex abuse.

The church has recognized that this issue has to be faced and Pope John Paul II has entered the debate on several occasions. His oft-repeated remark "celibacy is not essential to the priesthood" was quoted in both *Time* magazine and the *New York Times* in July 1993. But his statement refers to exceptions rather than the rule and has to be balanced against the official position of Catholic church officials, their psychiatrists and lawyers, which insists that there is no connection between mandatory celibacy and instances of clergy sexual abuse. The view was most recently enunciated when the pope met the Irish Catholic bishops in June 1999:

> At a time when priests are suffering due to the pressures of the surrounding culture and the terrible scandal given by some of their brother priests, it is essential to invite them to draw strength from a deeper insight into their priestly identity and mission...
>
> These scandals, and a sociological rather than theological concept of the church, sometimes lead to calls for a change in the discipline of celibacy.

However, we cannot overlook the fact that the church recognizes God's will through the interior guidance of the Holy Spirit and that the church's living tradition constitutes a clear affirmation of the consonance of celibacy, for profound theological and anthropological reasons, with the sacramental character of the priesthood. The difficulties involved in preserving chastity are not sufficient reasons for overturning the law of celibacy.

Critics of this view are found both within the Catholic church and outside it. They claim that it is not the overturning of celibacy which is the problem but the insistence on obligatory celibacy. No one will argue against the voluntary practice of celibacy, which is generally seen to be a helpful and creative discipline when it is undertaken without pressure by those who wish to adopt this life-style as a means to bringing them closer to God.

The complication comes when celibacy is made a forced requisite for the priestly life, because then it appears to create unresolvable tensions and a strong feeling of guilt and shame in those who are not able to maintain their celibate vows. This is especially so when the vow is made at a relatively young age.

Judging from surveys of the present situation, there appears to be a groundswell of Catholic opposition to celibacy developing among young priests. Estimates in 1987 claimed that the number of priests turning their backs on celibacy is about 6000 in Germany, 8000 in Italy and 8000 in France.[3] As shown earlier, in the year 2000 American Catholic commentators believe there could be at least 50 percent of priests in the United States of America who do not keep their celibacy vows. This would represent approximately 25,000 priests.

How do priests resolve the inner turmoil of publicly claiming one life-style when they want privately to live another? What solutions are open to them?

If we try to see this from the point of view of a hypothetical confused priest seeking resolution of his sexual drive, it is easy to see that the main possibility before him is to sexually abuse a child. He would not use these words and if he took this action he would persuade himself that he is merely having a close personal relationship with a child. But as this relationship developed, it would enable the priest to resolve his sexual drive with little or no risk of detection. To relate in this way to a child would certainly involve less threat than a personal relationship with an adult.

A priest has contact with dozens, or even hundreds, of children. He is expected to be friendly with children and to act as their friend and father figure. Most older people know that children are easily intimidated by an adult and can be manipulated into a compromising situation without much difficulty. Children have been taught to trust adults, especially one who has a dominant leadership role in the church or in the community. A priest also lives in an aura of privacy, with his study and vestry available as places where he can meet children and where abuse can take place without fear of interruption or detection.

The celibate priesthood can be an extremely lonely life and the hierarchical structure of the church will sometimes make the life of the priest competitive rather than cooperative. Priests need affection and friendship and the system does not provide much opportunity for meeting these needs. Seen in this context, it should not cause any surprise that the priest releases his inner tension by turning to children.

Of course, the priest we describe is not hypothetical. He is typical of numerous lonely celibates who seek fulfilment by breaking their vow of celibacy by having a sexual relationship with a minor. The quick survey in chapter 2 would suggest that he is in fact representative of several hundred clergy around the world, Catholic, Orthodox and Protestant, who have escaped the pressures and loneliness of the clerical life-style by developing a sexual relation with a child.

The church has been, and continues to be, an attractive place for child sex abusers to find refuge and the ministry of the church remains a good career option for a person with paedophile tendencies.

This has been confirmed by recent studies. Frank Valcour, the medical director at St Luke's Institute in Maryland, claims: "The sexually underdeveloped person may be drawn to a profession where celibacy is a given. The priesthood can be a safe place for such persons, where they will not be called upon to develop sexually – where, in fact, they may even be rewarded for not developing a sexual identity."[4] Jay R. Feierman, a psychiatrist at the University of New Mexico, has treated about five hundred abusive priests in 15 years. He says that the church invariably attracts a number of potential molesters and claims this is because of its rule on compulsory celibacy.

The issue of obligatory celibacy and its link with child sex abuse will continue to be debated and resolved within the Catholic church, as it is also being discussed in Buddhism, Hinduism and other religious groups where celibacy is a requirement for those aspiring to holy office.

Although some will claim there is a logical connection between celibacy and child sexual abuse, this does not explain abuse by ministers within Protestant and Orthodox churches. While the number of these abusers is proportionately less, the seriousness of their crimes is just as great.

Among Protestant churches, those described as theologically conservative appear to be the ones with the largest number of child sex abusers, and this may be related to the fact that in their attitudes to women and children they usually come closest to the Augustinian views of sexuality. Traditionally, they have been strongly patriarchal in their decision-making and ministry and their sermons are laced with emotive views which link human sexuality with sin. This is not universally true of conservative groups but certainly it has been a marked trait among the religious right in America.

Currently, there is a great deal of research being undertaken by police and behavioural psychologists to try and formulate a profile of sex abusers. Those searching for such behavioural clues have often noted the fact that a large number of the abusers claim to hold conservative Christian values.

A theology of sex

Within mainstream Protestant and Anglican churches the more common problem has been sexual harassment. While this is outside the purview of this book, it does reflect badly on our understanding of human sexuality and gives rise to the anxiety which church leaders feel (or should feel) about the overall attitude of the church towards sexual relationships.

If the church is to be faithful to the gospel, rather than the inherited burden of medieval practice, then it has to develop a more responsible theology of sex. Some of the components which would be included in this theology are the following:

– Sexual relationships must take place in an atmosphere where there is complete respect for the other person as an equal and where neither party has any superior rights over the other person by reason of sex, age or status.

– A theology of sexuality must deal honestly with the problem of power and the way this is used, both physically and psychologically, in relationships between the sexes and between individuals. In doing so it will seek to understand the example of Jesus who, though all-powerful, voluntarily chose the way of powerlessness in order to fulfil the will of God.

– There must be recognition of the emerging needs of children and young people, to ensure that their sexual needs are met in a manner which is appropriate to their healthy development.

– Greater compassion and understanding needs to be expressed for those who are, or have been, the victims of sexual abuse.

– The place of (mandatory) celibacy in the life of the church and/or as an option for Christians needs to be assessed.

– A sexual relationship between two consenting adults must never be automatically seen as dirty, degrading or sinful. Such a relationship should be described in positive terms and be understood as having the potential for a sacred act of union.

There are increasing signs that the seminaries of the churches are at last coming to terms with the need to give better instruction to those training for the ministry. Within some denominations, women are now presenting themselves for ministry in large numbers and this has ensured that patriarchal methods of instruction and patriarchal values being taught are both being challenged with vigour. The development of a more mature and responsible way of living with our sexuality is a strong sign of hope for the church of the future.

Our sexuality is a gift from God and therefore part of the beauty of being human. Like many of God's gifts it will bring great happiness if used wisely. But if the gift is used to exploit others, our sexuality will become a millstone permanently around our neck.

NOTES

[1] CWNews.com, 2 Feb. 2000.
[2] Tertullian, *On Female Dress*, quoted in Karen Armstrong, *A History of God*, New York, Ballantine, 1993, p.124.
[3] Quoted in Uta Ranke-Heinemann, *Eunuchs for the Kingdom of Heaven*, New York, Penguin, 1990, p.118.
[4] Paul Wilkes, in *The New Yorker*, 7 June 1993.

As this book was going to the printers (September 2001) a French court in Normandy found the bishop of Bayeaux, Pierre Pecan, guilty of perverting justice by concealing the crime of one of his paedophile priests (see p.32). He was given a three month suspended sentence. It is the first time a court has convicted a religious leader for concealing a crime admitted in the confessional. The precedent set by this case will have far-reaching effects on the practice of confession and forgiveness in many churches.

4. Who Are the Hidden Abusers?

Some simple definitions:

Paedophiles (pedophiles – USA) are adults with a persistent abnormal sexual attraction to a child.
Pederasts are paedophiles who are sexually attracted to boy children only.
Paraphilia is deviant sexual behaviour of which paedophilia is one.
Child in the United Nations convention means under the age of 18 years. But the age of consent in many countries is 16 years and some laws covering child sex abuse use this as the upper age limit of childhood.

To most people, the concept of paedophilia is totally repulsive. The idea that there could be men looking out of the window watching their children playing and planning how to sexually abuse them fills the average parent with horror. And when people discover that the minister or choirmaster at their own church has been abusing some of the young children within the church, they are aghast and become so totally enraged at the offender that they behave irrationally.

At some stage they will be asking each other: "What's wrong with these men? How can they do such things to innocent children? What gets into them that they want to seek out children as sexual partners?"

The same questions continue to perplex law enforcement officers, social workers and others who have to deal with paedophiles.

It would be comforting if we could find the reason for such behaviour, and even better if we could work out an accurate profile of the typical child sex offender. Unfortunately that is not possible from our present state of knowledge.

We do know that paedophiles are not usually the repugnant, unsavoury characters we meet in TV crime stories. Nor are they usually violent or macho men. It is uncommon, though not unknown, to find a paedophile who is sadistic, senile or mentally retarded. It is more usual to find that paedophiles are respected members of the community, active in the church and friendly with their neighbours. They are persons who are trusted and even loved by the whole community.

It is this outward lack of criminal characteristics that makes the crime they commit so hard to accept. It also makes it very difficult to compose a profile of the abuser. The key to their behaviour is still missing.

However, the experience of working with paedophiles may give some pointers to their psyche. Taken together, these pointers do not add up to a profile of abusers but they do provide a small portal to the hidden world of the persistent child sex abuser.

• *Paedophiles can come from any walk of life.*

Abusers can be politicians or film stars, lawyers or labourers, priests or plumbers. Paedophiles include men who are multi-millionaires and those who are unemployed. Paedophiles are anxious to remind people that many of the famous are included in their number. Lewis Carroll of *Alice in Wonderland* fame had a passion for taking photographs of young girls and is now claimed by the paedophile community as one of their own, though scholars are divided on the truth of this assertion. Paedophiles can be of any age, any nationality and either sex, but males far outnumber females. There is no single image that fits every situation.

• *Paedophiles prefer to work near children.*

The entire life-style of paedophiles revolves around the abuse of children, so they are always seeking new victims. This is the reason for selected occupations attracting a disproportionate number of paedophiles to their ranks. Teaching is an obvious choice for the abuser and is probably the most popular profession for paedophiles. Many of the religious abusers have been teachers in church schools.

The church has also been a favourite career choice for child sex abusers. It is possible that some paedophiles choose to enter the church for the right reason, hoping that the strict moral code would protect them from their inner drive to abuse children. But in reality, clergy have considerable freedom of action and access to children. When faced with temptation the paedophile often does not have the will to resist.

If their chosen career does not give easy access to children, paedophiles will often be active volunteers in youth organizations such as Boy Scouts, sports clubs or the YMCA.

- *Most paedophiles are "nice" people.*

This will seem, at first, to be an outrageous statement but it can easily be verified. The abuser is a predator. He has to win over the confidence of the child and in doing so will often have to convince the child's parents that he is a person to be trusted. Paedophiles can become so adept at being charming and nice that, even when one is convicted of a serious crime against a child, his friends and colleagues may still refuse to believe that he is really guilty. Abusers have trained themselves to be con-men. They will dress to impress and act in a way that gives them credibility with their associates. They will go to extraordinary lengths to ingratiate themselves with the parents of children they want to abuse. There are even cases of a paedophile marrying so that he can gain access to his wife's own young children or to the children of her friends.

When paedophiles are brought to court and faced with their crimes, there are almost always people who will give a positive character reference to the abuser. He is a really "nice" man.

- *Paedophiles specialize.*

Most persistent abusers have a fixation on a particular age and sex. Some will abuse only boys (pederasts) and some only girls. A few abuse both.

The age of the child is significant to the abuser. For some reason, the serial paedophile usually becomes locked in to a particular age group and will seek victims in that age group only. He will define and identify his victims in terms of physical characteristics, such as body hair or pre-pubescence, and will have no interest in a sexual relationship outside that narrow range.

Serial paedophiles are usually more oriented to younger children and especially pre-pubescent children, either boys or girls. It is not uncommon for a paedophile to have a fixation on (for example) 11- or 12-year-old girls and abuse a single child regularly for a short time until she gets too old, then reject her and seek another victim.

• *Paedophiles are predators.*

When they talk about children, the language used by paedophiles in correspondence and in conversation is couched in the tribal language of the hunter. They stalk their prey and plan their hunt with meticulous care. If they have a particular child in their sights, they will show enormous patience in cultivating that child and obtaining as much information as possible so that they can plan their final attack.

It appears that some paedophiles get such an adrenalin rush from hunting and finally "capturing their prey" that this becomes their major activity. Once they have abused the child they immediately seek another victim and begin the grooming and planning process all over again.

• *The paedophile identifies with his "prey".*

Paedophiles are extremely knowledgeable about current youth culture. They can tell you the names of all the songs young people are listening to, they will know all the teenage jargon and which things are "cool" for the teens. In many cases a paedophile will convert a room of his home into a playing area to attract children of the age he prefers. He will stock it with dolls or trains, play stations or magazines, and a selection of toys appropriate to the age of the child he is trying to seduce. It is a major part of the grooming process as he seeks to win the confidence of the child.

• *Paedophiles are collectors.*

The analogy with hunting continues. The paedophile wants to have a trophy of the hunt. Their trophy is often in the form of a photograph of the child who has been abused or even a video clip of the actual abuse. In the days when technology was less advanced, many paedophiles kept long and meticulous written records of the children they had abused. They also kept records of other paedophiles and sometimes the capture of a long-time paedophile meant the uncovering of written records that exposed the names and activities of a number of other paedophiles.

In the modern world the internet provides a new, and unfortunately growing, source of child sex material for paedophiles.

- *Paedophiles seek the lonely and the vulnerable.*

With many parents working, there is less time for them or for other care-givers to spend time with children and assist in their development. If the child cannot develop the social skills needed to relate to peers, he or she will live a lonely and sometimes unhappy childhood. Paedophiles become expert at identifying such vulnerable children and act to fill the vacuum in the child's life. The caring and apparently compassionate adult can become the child's first experience with an adult who will listen to their problems and shower gifts and affection upon them.

Of course, not all the paedophiles' victims are lonely children. Many children are attracted to a paedophile by a sense of adventure or strong sexual curiosity. The paedophile has learned from experience how to be an expert in identifying the psyche of the child.

- *Paedophiles are obsessed.*

The fixation of paedophiles on children becomes obsessive. It dominates their thinking, their actions, their marriage (or non-marriage), their career path, their hobbies and their entire life-style.

The development of the internet has provided individual paedophiles with a wider network of like-minded people and has fed their obsessive behaviour. Members of paedophile clubs who have been arrested tell stories of the way they stay awake night after night speaking with other members around the world. They tell of reaching a point where they could think of nothing else. It filled all their waking moments and seemingly many members tried to outdo the others with graphic pictures and stories of child sex abuse.

The art of deception

These are some of the characteristics which have been observed in paedophiles but they are not enough to enable us to isolate the paedophile from the wider community. Since the paedophile is, by choice, a highly secretive person, especially in relation to his sexual activities, most outsiders will have difficulty recognizing the symptoms of his deviant behaviour in his daily life. The private life of the paedophile is always carefully hidden from colleagues and neighbours.

Many of the characteristics of paedophiles are shared by other members of the public. Obviously, many teachers and clergy and scout masters care passionately about children without having the least desire to abuse them. A genuine concern and compassion for children is one of the saintly virtues. The paedophile builds on this community attitude and can even be praised for the work he does for children.

When the Mormon elder Mark Morgan opened a home for street children in Bangkok, visiting Mormon businessmen heard about his work and raised large sums of money to support what he was doing. Glowing articles about him appeared in Mormon newsletters in the United States, but the illusion was shattered when the police arrested Morgan for child abuse and placed him in prison. His association with the North American Man-Boy Love Association (NAMBLA) was exposed and Morgan slipped from sainthood to imprisonment.

None of this brings us closer to understanding the compulsion which drives the paedophile, nor the origins of his deviant behaviour.

But there are some small clues. We know that the life of the paedophile is a long chapter of subterfuge, secrecy and double standards. The paedophile is aware that the community at large does not condone his behaviour, so in his anxiety to continue his obsession he has to develop many strategies to avoid detection. Such behaviour is possibly learned at a quite early age. When other young teens like him are dating girls or keeping company with their peers, the potential paedophile finds no erotic excitement in a peer relationship. Instead, he may become sexually aroused at the sight of a young child having a bath. It is unlikely he would share these feelings with anyone else but if he did so he would be ridiculed and bullied.

Out of such experiences the young paedophile realizes that he is different from many of his peers and takes great pains to keep his sex life completely private from any public scrutiny. As he becomes older he masters the art of deception. He tries to establish himself as a good and upright citizen, which usually means conforming to the conservative political and religious norms of his time.

This has considerable implications for the church. In the recent past, regular attendance at church and participation in its activities was seen as a mark of respectability. But it also provides a good cover for the paedophile, and one loses count of the number of times court records of paedophiles state that the defendant is an active church member.

For some time, there was an assumption that child sex abusers were just repeating a pattern and had themselves been abused as a child. It is true that many abusers were victims of abuse when they were children but this is by no means always the case. Studies have shown a wide divergence in the percentage of offenders who have been abused as children. It is equally true that many men who were sexually abused as children do not become paedophiles. While it may be a significant factor in the case of some adult abusers, it is not a universal explanation.

Sex and power

When you have lived with the impact of child sex abuse for some time, you realize that a crucial element in understanding what is taking place is contained in the word "power". Paedophilia has nothing to do with "philia" (love) but a great deal to do with power.

At the core of the everyday relationships and actions of many people lies the search for power. Seldom named and little understood, this fact may provide some more clues to our knowledge of child sex abuse.

Many sexual relationships are best understood in terms of power. When a group of young teenage boys look at a similar group of young girls the conversation about sex revolves around statements of power. A successful relationship is described as "a conquest" and it is assumed it will provide status and power among peers. Even when the encounter is expressed in romantic language, the end result is one of dominance. The sexual act enables the person to assert some dominance over another person and within the peer group.

We may be able to see child sex abuse better if it is understood in terms of power. There is no clearer illustration of complete power and dominance than when an adult has a sexual relationship with a child. In whatever terms you describe it, the adult is almost totally powerful and the child almost totally powerless. The adult has the power of physical strength, of psychological understanding, of money, of knowledge, of supporting networks, of influence and of age. When the abuser is a pastor or church leader, he can (and shamefully sometimes does) call on the additional power of God.

All child sex abuse is a misuse of power and authority but when it is performed by a religious leader is takes on a dangerous dimension. The priest stands in the place of God and speaks with the whole force of the religious institution behind him. On behalf of God, the priest claims authority to pronounce the forgiveness of sin. If a priest with an overwhelming sexual urge uses this power, it becomes almost impossible for a young person to resist.

What power does a child have against such overwhelming odds? Paedophiles regularly claim that young people are anxious to have sex with an adult and are the ones to make the first overtures. Paedophiles pretend that they were only giving in to the pleading of the child for sex and they did it to please the child.

Such rationalizations carry little conviction when seen against the power advantages of the adult over the few resources of the child.

Some interesting insights came from studies conducted on behalf of ECPAT International as preparation for the first World Congress against Commercial Sexual Exploitation of Children, held in Stockholm in August 1996. Two British sociologists were commissioned to study child sex tourism in a number of tourist destinations. Their reports on seven destinations are full of quotes by sex abusers which reveal, to some extent, the part which power and the desire to control plays in their activities.

> Almost all the sex tourists interviewed spoke with great bitterness about white women's power to deny them sexual access. Macho lads complained that English women are "hard work" and that going to discos in England is "a waste of time". In short, sex tourists express a kind of misogynous rage against women who have the power to demand anything at all – whether it is the right to have a say over who they have sex with and when, or the right to maintain payments for the children.
>
> As well as attaining power over the material world and over women, these men experience a greater sense of power over their own bodies in Thailand, certainly as far as their sexuality is concerned... Finally, sex tourism gives sex tourists a sense of power over other men. The fact that they are in a position to have sex with as many "beautiful women" as they want makes them feel "one up" on the men who stay at home.[1]

Several of the reports alluded to the fact that many sex tourists were physically and socially unattractive men who possessed little real power and received little respect in their home country. The allure of a sex tourist destination in a developing country was that they could be reinvigorated by the power they had over the lives of teenage girls and children and could feel wanted and loved.

One possible conclusion from these findings may be that many paedophiles are men who have been rejected and not respected by their peers in early life and who carry that sense of inadequacy with them into later life. In seeking control they turn to the most vulnerable in society, the children, and exploit them.

It is only a partial answer to a puzzling situation to suggest that the desire for power and dominance is a driving factor in the desire of some men to sexually abuse children. At best we can say it may be one more piece in the jigsaw puzzle of child sex abuse.

NOTE

[1] From Report 7-*Thailand*, a research paper by Julia O'Connell Davidson and Jacqueline Sanchez Taylor, Department of Sociology, University of Leicester, UK, for ECPAT International, 1994.

5. Avoiding the Issue

Hiding things was one stratagem
in a psychology of power rooted in fear...

Despite a noble history of voluntary celibacy,
too many bishops – shut off from affective bonding,
unlettered in the vocabulary of child raising,
swamped by homosexuality and pederasty, hiding
behind lawyers, mired in the muck of the media –
were blinded by their flaw
and disgraced the people of God.[1]

Until recently, the issue of child sex abuse had probably never been raised in creeds or in church teaching on morals or ethics. Like the rest of society, the church did not want to know that adults were sexually abusing children. Whenever a case was uncovered it was soon pushed away out of sight.

If the question should arise from time to time, the church would be certain to speak firmly against a sexual relationship between an adult and a child. That much is clear. The Didache, an early church teaching text which dates from about 120 A.D., states bluntly: "Thou shalt not seduce young boys" (II:2).

The problem is not with official statements of the church. Naturally they will always be strongly opposed to the sexual abuse of a child. The greatest difficulty emerges when the church has to deal with the issue in the glare of publicity.

Historically, the church once existed as a parallel state, with its own rules, laws and regulations alongside those of the government. In this position of privilege the church was able to defend itself from its enemies and often has been strong enough to bring kings and emperors to their knees. Many of the inherited structures in the church retain those old hierarchical concepts, even though the power that is expressed in them today is more illusory than real.

There are still a few places where the church retains the power successfully to challenge the state, as it has done recently in the Philippines when the church supported and encouraged people's movements to overthrow political leaders. But such events are rare. The church today rarely wields any strong political or economic power that is effective enough to bring major changes in society.

The days of church power may have gone but the mindset has not. Much re-education will be required if the church is to deal with charges of clergy abuse in a less defensive manner and in a way which will restore community confidence in its integrity.

The church retains a powerful internal sub-culture with its own unique customs of secrecy and cohesion. When one of its clergy is accused by secular authorities of committing a crime such as child sex abuse or sexual harassment, the church closes ranks very quickly.

Many sex abuse survivors have a legitimate grievance against the church because of its failure to respond to the warning signals that were given. Over the past thirty years, numerous cases of child sex abuse by clergy have been brought to the attention of church authorities but the church either ignored them or responded in an inappropriate manner. This has enabled the abuser to continue to act in a predatory manner and to abuse more children. As the facts have come to the surface many Christians have been shocked by the unpalatable truth that not only has one of their ministers sexually abused a child but that church leaders have tried to conceal the facts or have shown duplicity in dealing with the authorities.

We have to confess that the church has not handled these situations with the sensitivity required. Rather, the record of church authorities would suggest that the chief preoccupation of the church has been to try and make the whole problem go away. Consider the way some churches have reacted.

• *By hiding the evidence*

Documents in trials in the USA have uncovered the fact that bishops have in some cases recommended the shredding of personal files on priests lest they could be used as evidence in law-suits.[2]

- *By minimizing the seriousness of the abuse*

Reviewing abuse cases, Paul Wilkes has commented that young victims were sometimes viewed as inanimate objects or were looked upon as sources of temptation for a consecrated servant of God. One archbishop said, "They're kids, they don't know anything about sex, they'll forget about it."[3] The response of the archbishop shows little understanding of both the rights and the sensitivities of a child when he assumes that being sexually abused is a minor event and something that a child will soon forget.

- *By shifting the blame to the children*

Bishop Rembert Weakland of Milwaukee is quoted as saying of the children who were abused that they are "sexually very active, aggressive and often quite streetwise". An anonymous bishop was quoted as saying, "Young boys recover from this type of thing very quickly if people don't make a big thing out of it."

- *By shifting the blame to another organization*

"You should be aware that Brother Z was appointed by the diocese to the position of principal... We do not suggest the diocese has any liability either [but] the first point we make is that there was no employer-employment relationship in our view at the time of the abuse."[4]

- *By shifting the blame to the media*

Regarding the papal letter to American bishops some of the reporters were accused of aggravating the situation by sensational reporting: "While acknowledging the right to freedom of information, one cannot acquiesce in treating moral evil as an occasion for sensationalism."

- *By shifting the blame to the world*

Joaquin Navarro-Vails, a spokesman for the Vatican, wrote to bishops in the United States after a number of major scandals: "One would have to ask if the real culprit is not a society that is irresponsibly permissive, hyper-inflated with sexuality (and) capable of creating circumstances that induce even people who have received a solid moral foundation to commit grave moral acts."

Speaking the truth

The case of Rudolph Kos, a priest in Texas, referred to in chapter 2, which led to the court awarding a record US$120 million in damages, shows how tragically the church has sometimes misread the situation.

As early as 1985, a number of priests had expressed concern to the Catholic personnel board in Dallas about Father Kos's habit of bringing boys to spend the night with him in his room at the vestry. The boys were aged between 9 and 18 years. Further complaints by priests followed in 1986 and again in 1991. Each complaint was ignored by the board, which instead promoted Kos from assistant pastor to pastor.

Early in 1992 a social worker advised church officials that all the evidence pointed to Kos being "a textbook paedophile".

Even then it was another year before the diocese suspended Kos from performing his duties and it was only the growing threat of law-suits which prompted them to act. By that time it was too late for former altar boy Jay Lemberger, who had committed suicide – an action which has been linked to the abuse he had suffered from Kos.

To the Texas public, the actions of the diocese suggested that fear of scandal far exceeded their concern for the abused boys. The *Los Angeles Times* reports attorney Richard Johnson as saying, "Their main concern in the early years was 'God forbid anyone should know'." Once the media had the story of Kos running, it was undoubtedly made worse by the ineptitude of the church in handling the accusations

The way the diocese dealt with the media is typical of similar events in the church all round the world.

There is no doubt the church has been totally unprepared for the spate of abuse accusations made in the past decade. In a controlled environment, the church could well have used its power and influence to ensure that it was not accountable for the problem, but in the more open society of recent years the possibility of cover-up had become much less.

Certainly the media builds up these stories with great enthusiasm. But in contemporary society it is part of the role of the media to expose injustice and crime. The fact that the crime takes place in an organization which has generally been seen as morally and ethically clean gives an undoubted edge to the reporting and could even be seen as an inverted compliment to the church. The community expects better of the Christian community and through these reports is demanding more accountability.

Some instruction in good public relations must be on the future agenda for leaders of the church. And the first lesson has to be the need for transparent honesty. Speaking the truth is its own witness.

NOTES

[1] Jason Berry, *Lead Us Not Into Temptation*, New York, Doubleday, 1992.
[2] *Newsweek*, 16 Aug. 1993.
[3] Paul Wilkes, in *The New Yorker*, 7 June 1993.
[4] Lawyer's letter to the prosecutor in a court case.

6. Seeking Solutions

Twenty years ago it was just a puzzle,
it was such a shock and surprise.
It was very much a hidden phenomenon
and a hidden crime.
But I think nowadays these things
are much more understood.
We obviously have been on a steep learning curve.[1]

Perhaps the worst is over for the church.

Many of the past actions of the church are reflections of the same kind of response which used to take place in schools, youth organizations or any other group faced with a paedophile in their midst. Much was done in ignorance. There is some truth in the suggestion that society itself carries some responsibility, since the whole community colluded in a pact of silence about child sex abuse. It was not an issue in the media until a few years ago.

Once some facts about child sex abuse came into the open the church was slow to respond, and in some of the reactions listed in the last chapter church authorities showed a naivety and lack of professionalism which brought a strong backlash from the media and the community. Hopefully, some important lessons have been learned.

Most major churches around the world have been galvanized into action by the media attention given to sexual abuse of children by clergy. There is a realization that immediate change in church procedures and protocols must be made and these are gradually being put in place by most major churches.

Christians are naturally distressed at the reality of sexual abuse by members of the church. They need to be equally concerned at the general growth of child sex abuse in the world.

In 1989 several Christian organizations based in Asia were disturbed to read reports that young children were being sold for sex in countries like Thailand and the Philippines. Through the initiative of the Ecumenical Coalition on Third World Tourism, based in Bangkok, research was organized by the council of churches in the Philippines, Sri Lanka, Thailand and Taiwan. The findings were presented to a small consultation in May 1990 and sent shock waves around the world.

Their studies showed that an estimated one million children under the age of 16 years were being kept as child sex slaves in brothels in Asia alone. Equally startling was the discovery that a large part of the increased demand for child sex was the result of paedophile tourists coming to Asia from Western countries specifically for that purpose.[2]

As a result of the 1990 conference, an international organization was set up to combat this trade in children. Originally called ECPAT (End Child Prostitution in Asian Tourism), it made its headquarters in Bangkok and centred its activities in Asia. Initial funding for its work came from church mission agencies in Europe and Australia.

The organization moved quickly beyond its original church base. While a few people were interested in retaining the programme as a purely Christian service agency, most of the planners realized that the enormity of the problem meant that any proper solution would involve as wide a section of the population as possible. It was immediately clear that social change in countries such as Thailand, Sri Lanka and India required the full participation of Buddhists and Hindus. ECPAT became religiously and politically inclusive.

Today, after ten years, the organization has outgrown its Asian roots and has member organizations in more than fifty countries in all continents. Its mandate has also broadened to include child pornography and trafficking in children for sexual purposes. It has been successful in forcing governments to introduce new laws and to strengthen law enforcement against abusers. The issues are of sufficient importance that they have united conservatives and liberals with people of many different religious backgrounds in a common campaign to end the commercial sexual exploitation of children.

Recognition and positive developments

The battle to protect children from abuse continues. Are we winning?

There have been many successes. On the local scene there is now a far greater recognition of the reality of child sex abuse. Paedophiles can no longer operate with the impunity they once knew. Many churches and youth organizations have introduced protocols which cover the behaviour of their leaders and which can be strictly enforced.

And we are not as naïve as we used to be. Stories told by victims of abuse who have spoken publicly have provided us with a clear picture of the long-term damage done to the psyche of a child by sexual abuse. The memory of feeling shame, guilt and pain is carried with them for the rest of their life.

Also important is the fact that the growing visibility of the problem has led to the development of many new community services. For the victims of abuse there are now specialized counselling services and well-organized victim support groups. For the abuser there are many types of programmes aimed at rehabilitating or attempting to cure the abuser of his desire to abuse children. While these programmes have had only partial success, they are a beginning in our efforts to stop the growth in abuse.

Other developments have also been positive. The judiciary and law-makers have begun to realize the seriousness of the crime and have introduced more effective penalties. Law enforcement agencies are now giving the abuse of children more specialized attention. New laws to protect children, including extraterritorial laws, have been approved in many countries.

The threat of the internet

But just as it appeared that things were starting to improve, those working to end the sexual abuse of children have come face-to-face with a daunting new enemy – the internet.

Of course, the internet is a wonderful and exciting development and it will continue to enrich our lives in unexpected new ways. We now have instant access to the wisdom of the world and can relate to individuals and groups in every corner of the planet. It is transforming our lives.

At the same time, the internet has given child sex abusers a wonderful new way to continue their activities and to extend them beyond anything previously possible. Three features of the internet have special appeal to the abuser:

• The anonymity of the internet means that a paedophile can speak directly to other paedophiles around the world in relative privacy. Monitoring by the police of conversations and messages is illegal in some countries and is not conducted on a large scale in others. If paedophiles use encryption, the possibility of their messages being discovered becomes less.

This line of communication is of great importance to the paedophile. Its advantages will be obvious. Perhaps the main one is that it provides a giant validating mechanism for the paedophile's way of life. Paedophiles are always trying to justify their actions and now they can convince themselves more easily that they are right. They rationalize their behaviour: "Sure, the people around here don't understand me, but look at all these people in other parts of the world who act like me. What we are doing is good for the kids, helping them to experience real love from a caring adult. It is only this up-tight society that doesn't understand children's needs." Sharing this kind of view on the internet helps to entrench the behaviour of the paedophile.

Anonymity also provides an invaluable source of private information. Paedophiles learn from each other new ways to avoid the law and how to entice children. Best of all for them, they discover the tourist destinations which are safe for child sex abusers. They can learn where to go in Thailand, Nicaragua or Kenya to find children. They will be told where to stay, who to meet and how much everything will cost. If they are part of a paedophile network they can arrange gatherings of like-minded friends in a tourist country and share their experiences.

• The second advantage of the internet for abusers is that they can share actual examples of abuse by exchanging child pornography and experiences. As we noted, paedophiles have always been avid collectors and some of them amass large quantities of child pornography. The internet provides them with a quick, cheap and easy way to build up huge collections of pornography and to exchange these with other paedophiles around the world. Police arresting child pornographers are often amazed at the size of the files on the paedophile's computer. In some cases, they download tens of thousands of images.

The content of some pictures and video clips is appalling. The cruelty of the acts and the vicious way they are perpetrated on quite young children has meant that police and others who have to view such material later need to undertake counselling for secondary trauma.

We must remind ourselves that the internet is still in its infancy and that it will have even more surprises in store for us. One new development that must be of great concern is the use of videos attached to computers to provide real-time images of abuse. There have been two recent instances of this activity uncovered by police.

The Orchid Club exposed in 1998 and the Wonderland Club which was broken in 2001 were small paedophile associations. The first was based in the United States and the second in England, though its members were found in 21 countries of the world. Entry to the club was strictly monitored and the members were so security conscious that it took a whole series of initiation tests and passwords before entry was assured.

Members of the two groups all ended up with computers overflowing with child pornography, including many explicit videos. From time to time one of the members would abuse a child at a pre-arranged time and would have the other members of the club watching in real time. Those computers which enabled a spoken network as well gave opportunity for the other members watching to give encouragement or make suggestions.

More than one hundred people were arrested in the Wonderland Club sting and this yielded an astonishing cache of over 750,000 explicit photos of child pornography with children as young as 18 months.

The quantum of child pornographic material on the net is increasing at a rapid rate. It is important to remind ourselves that behind almost all of these images there is a real child. Each day there are children somewhere in the world who are being sexually abused and, at the same time, filmed on a video camera. The trauma of their abuse has been recorded in perpetuity. It will always be somewhere on the net and no matter how well the abused child is counselled, when he or she becomes an adult the knowledge that there are paedophiles in other places watching the abuse again and again and again becomes a huge burden for any person to carry. You do not need to ask why some abused children commit suicide when they are in their teens.

• There is one further advantage of the internet for predatory abusers. They can search for children to abuse and cultivate their friendship before arranging to meet face to face. Paedophiles no longer have to sit in a car outside a school watching to see if they can find a possible victim; now they hunt their victims in the safety of their own homes.

Their strategy is deceptively simple. They enter chat rooms on the internet and pretend to be a boy or girl of the same age as the child they want to molest. As noted before, they already know the language of the children, the films they will be watching and the music they enjoy. The process of grooming their victim begins and it becomes increasingly explicit as messages are exchanged.

In some cases, a paedophile will arrange a meeting in a quiet or isolated place. There have been several cases of this nature documented and some of these meetings have had serious consequences for the child.

It is of great importance that all parents be made aware of this process and that they help their children to practise internet safety. Under no circumstances should children give their home address to a stranger on the internet and they should never arrange to meet a stranger outside the security of their own home.

Learning in crisis

Those who work to stop the sexual abuse of children are winning and losing at the same time. Sexual abuse of children is now better understood and therefore better able to be challenged and, hopefully, ended. The number of children kept as prostitutes in some countries has declined because of stricter law enforcement, but as this happens other countries become more popular destinations for sex tourists. It is worth noting that in countries which have become more economically developed, child prostitution appears to be less of a problem, but when war and poverty escalate the problem becomes greater. Technology has helped us develop new ways to know what is happening around the world with regard to child abuse, but it has increased the possibility of children becoming further victimized.

The church is winning and losing too. Negative publicity has forced a complete re-evaluation of the church's protocols and policies towards child sex abuse, and future generations of children will be protected more effectively from those who would abuse them. At the same time, the publicity has also caused the church to lose credibility in the eyes of many of its supporters.

As the Chinese proverb has it, a crisis is a mixture of danger and opportunity. If the church can learn from recent experiences and show a greater sensitivity to children and an increased awareness of its own weakness, then it will gain from the experiences of the last few years.

NOTES

[1] Archbishop Vincent Nichols, Birmingham.
[2] K. Srisang, ed., *Caught in Modern Slavery*, Bangkok, ECTWT, 1991.

7. Jesus Loves the Children

Jesus loves each little child;
Bring the children to his arms;
He will keep them safe from harm.[1]

On the few occasions recorded in the gospels when Jesus referred to children, it was always in a positive and protective way. When his followers wanted to know who was the most important person in heaven, Jesus called a child to him and reminded the followers that children are central to an understanding of the faith: "Whoever welcomes a child like this in my name, welcomes me" (Matt. 18:1-5). Later, the disciples tried to prevent the children from crowding close to Jesus but he insisted that they should be allowed to come to him – "to such as these belongs the kingdom of heaven" (Luke 18:15). The incident must have made an impression on the disciples because it is repeated in each of the first three gospels. Mark goes further and says that Jesus became angry with the disciples at the way they were treating the children (Mark 10:14).

The heart of the gospel is found in this encounter of Jesus with children. In it he calls the adult followers to learn from the children and to become like little children. This is not the same as asking them to become childish.

Among the chief characteristics of childhood are simplicity, trust and spontaneous joy. When Christ calls us to be like children, it is virtues such as these which adult Christians are called to embrace.

It is difficult to live in a complex world with a simple faith and a positive belief in those we meet but the few people who manage to capture it, like Mother Teresa in Calcutta, become role models for everyone.

Being innocent and trusting are dangerous concepts for adults in a world where so many want to cheat and lie and take advantage of other people. Finding people we can trust and places where we can be ourselves are gifts that are greatly needed.

Perhaps most of all we need to recapture that wonderful sense of awe and wonder which enables children to enjoy

God's creation, to laugh at butterflies and to be one with the universe in joy and hope.

The sad fact is that these virtues of childhood are exactly the ones which a child abuser will manipulate to bring a child under his influence.

Immediately after the blessing of children, the gospels record one of the strongest comments of Jesus's ministry.

> If anyone should cause one of these little ones to lose their faith in me, it would be better for that person to have a large mill-stone tied around his neck and be drowned in the deep sea. How terrible for the world that there are things that make people lose their faith! Such things will always happen but how terrible for the one who causes them! (Matt. 18:6,7)

The compassion and love which Jesus showed towards the children who came to him and the obvious care he had for their well-being is counterbalanced by his anger at adults who, selfishly and without care, abuse the trust of children.

It is a particularly blunt and emphatic statement being made. It is a passage to challenge the church and is regularly quoted when there is a case of a clergyman sexually abusing a child. There is a clear note of extreme anger in the words of Jesus. To sin against a young child has to be ranked by Christians as one of the worst crimes any person can commit.

Expressions of survival

Those of us who have seen its effects know that the sexual abuse of the young child is as bad as sin can get. Society ranks murder among the worst of crimes because the perpetrator is destroying another life. But in the sexual abuse of a young child a life is also being destroyed. It is a form of slow and living death which can stretch over many years. Murder is a terrible crime with a finality that shocks us but child sex abuse, especially when accompanied by violence, also destroys a life.

Fortunately, this worst-case scenario does not always happen. Some children are resilient enough to survive sexual abuse and subsequently are able to lead relatively full and creative lives. But there are many thousands of people whose whole life has been destroyed by unsought sexual abuse by an adult. These are usually the silent survivors. Until recently there was no place for them to go for healing or to share their experience with others. Today they form survivor groups in every large city and through the internet.

Survivors share their feelings through poetry and stories which make harrowing reading. It is clear that people who have been sexually abused by a minister or other religious leader feel a double betrayal. They have been betrayed by an adult they had trusted but, even worse, they have been betrayed by the church which is symbolized in the person of the minister. A single act of abuse may possibly distort their view of Christian faith for the rest of their days.

Listen to the expression of loneliness and betrayal felt by of one young Australian who was a survivor of clergy abuse:

Why have you forsaken me?
Trapped by betrayal
Why have you forsaken me
Violated by manipulation
Why have you forsaken me
Sacred objects used abused me
Why have you forsaken me
Rituals confused contorted
Why have you forsaken me
Searing alienation tearing degradation
Why have you forsaken me
Vicious bitter silent tears
Why have you forsaken me
Tortured derided, silent-still
Why have you forsaken me
Isolated desolation of innocence
Why have you forsaken me
Madness a refuge the cost easy to bear
Why have you forsaken me
Imprinted by another's mind and will
Why have you forsaken me
Mutilation and self-destruction
Why have you forsaken me

Body abused mind raped
Why have you forsaken me
Coerced by vulnerability
Why have you forsaken me
Humanity charity pity all unknown
I used to pray
Where were you then?[2]

The poem expresses the agony of just one young person who was a victim of someone who claimed to be ordained by God. What happens to the perception of the church when we multiply that a hundred times or a thousand times?

How do we measure the impact of a priest in New Bedford, United States of America, who admitted to having sexually abused at least 200 minors and during whose trial it was noted that at least 12 of his victims had attempted to commit suicide. "How terrible," said Jesus, "for the one who causes such things to happen."

NOTES

[1] Chinese hymn, Tzu-chen Chao.
[2] D.P. Irvine, Aug.-Sept. 1996.

8. Protecting the Child

We are guilty of many errors and many faults,
but our worst crime is abandoning the children,
neglecting the fountain of life.
Many things can wait, the children cannot.
Right now is the time their bones are being formed,
their senses being developed.
To them we cannot answer tomorrow.
Their name is today.
(Gabriela Mistral, Chile)

The past decade has been a bad one for the church. The chronicle of clergy abuse and the extent to which the church has participated in its cover-up is out of step with the high moral standards of Christianity. Whatever the actual extent of the abuse, the public perception of Christianity as a righteous community has suffered.

In February 1996, Philip Jenkins of Pennsylvania State University wrote a rather defensive book called *Pedophiles and Priests* in which he claimed that the issue of clergy sex abuse had been greatly exaggerated. He stated his belief that priest-paedophilia cases are extremely rare and that most of the sex abuse cases by clergy took place between homosexual priests and 16-17 year old boys, a crime which he implies is of lesser importance than the sexual abuse of a pre-pubescent child. He defends celibacy by claiming that "non-celibate clergy are just as likely to abuse" and adds that the figures for child sexual abuse and paedophilia are similar for clergy in denominations that do not enforce celibacy, although he does not provide any statistical evidence to confirm these statements.

It would be comforting for the church to believe the truth of some of these assertions, but in the six years since Jenkins's book was written it would be difficult to find any objective research that would substantiate the claims he makes. Clergy continue to be brought before the courts on child sex abuse cases and huge payments continue to be made to victims of this abuse.

Some people will suggest that the church is no worse than other sectors of society in child sex abuse and in dealing with its effects. This may or may not be true but that is not the point. The church preaches the virtues of respect and honesty and family values, so society has the right to expect that the church will be better than the rest of society in its moral conduct and will provide some leadership in ethical matters.

This was illustrated by a quite extraordinary case which uncovered a paedophile clergyman in Durham, England. Adrian McLaren, described as a "fine parish priest", not only abused a number of children but also filmed himself doing it. It took four police seven months to catalogue his huge collection of child pornography.

How did the police catch the priest? One day when he was away, his house was ransacked by burglars and they were so horrified to see the amount of pornography in the priest's study that they rang the police and gave them the tip-off which led to the priest's arrest. There may be honour among thieves but not between thieves and paedophiles.

In the church we have been so successful at preaching pious sermons on love and compassion that it is not surprising that the community expects us to match our words with our actions.

While it is true that in this book we have been speaking about a minority of clergy and we are talking about a small number of children in relation to the total population of children, that is not the point. Christianity has always placed great emphasis on the importance of every individual. According to the teaching of Jesus, the love of God towards each of us is such that even the hairs of our head are numbered. And since the eye of God is on the sparrow and not one of them is forgotten by God, surely God's care for people is assured. The absolute importance of each individual is summed up in these teachings from Christ's Sermon on the Mount.

The reality is that one child who is sexually abused is one too many.

The sexual abuse of each single child:
– is a moment of suffering for all people;
– a denial of our humanity;

– a rejection of our own future;
– and an attempt to destroy the beauty of God's creation.

The sexual abuse of a child by a priest is all of these plus a denial of his own public vows and an indictment on the whole Christian community. It is a call for repentance.

When child abuse cases were exposed in Newfoundland, Canada, Archbishop Alphonsus Penney resigned and spoke publicly to the church and to the children who had been abused:

> We are a sinful church... Our anger, our pain, our anguish, our shame and our vulnerability are clear to the whole world... We are sorry for the times you were not believed, were not supported or were ostracized in any way by the community. For every word and action which has deepened your pain, we are profoundly sorry.

The experiences that churches have gone through in this past decade have been a salutary lesson to each one of us. We have not served the children in our care as we ought to have done. We must learn from this and find ways of restitution.

Growing up in this complex new world is not an easy journey for our children and they need the best love and protection we can give them.

To abuse the trust of a child
is the greatest sin we can conceive
To love and protect a child is the finest gift we have to offer.

Appendix
Church Protocols

Churches will have different ways of dealing with the issue of child sex abuse according to their national laws and the ecclesiology and structure of their church.

There are some general guidelines in the establishment of protocols:

The victims
- All accusations of child sex abuse must be treated seriously and investigated thoroughly by competent persons who are trained for such work.
- Churches must ensure they have suitable personnel and places where accusations of abuse can be reported in confidence.
- Counselling services are required for both the victim of abuse and the victim's family.

Assessment of the crime
- A recognized consultative and advisory process will need to be established to hear any complaints against church leaders or members who are accused of child sex abuse.
- Where there is a suspicion of a criminal act the police will be notified as a matter of course.
- The church will cooperate fully with the civil authorities responsible for investigating allegations of sexual misconduct. They will not hide or mislead such authorities.

Informing the church community
- When the abuse is established and involves a church leader, there needs to be some public explanation to the church of what has occurred and an opportunity given for some response.
- Programmes of healing and understanding will be required.

Reinstatement of ministry
- When a minister of the church has been found guilty of the sexual abuse of a minor, he must never again be permitted to return to an unsupervised parish ministry or a ministry that includes access to minors.

Acceptance of an offender
- When a person who is known to have committed a sex offence against children seeks to renew membership in the church, he should be received with openness but with strict reservations. Some churches require the member to sign a written contract which gives the conditions under which he will exercise his membership in the church.

Appointment of clergy
- Stricter guidelines are required to screen persons seeking ordination to the ministry *before* they begin training. Those responsible for the training of clergy must ensure that the education of their students includes a full understanding of the need for proper moral behaviour towards children.
- Clergy need to understand that they must not cross sexual boundaries in any counselling or professional relationship.

Appointment of missionaries
- The appointment of missionaries, both clerical and lay, must also include appropriate psychological tests and interviews to ensure that the candidate does not have a tendency towards sexual misconduct with children. Where there is a police register of child sex abusers, the church should seek the opportunity to consult the register and obtain a clearance for the missionary candidates.

Education of the people
- Church members need to be aware of their responsibility to make the church a safe environment for children.